RECORDED VERSIONS
GUITAR

AUTHENTIC TRANSCRIPTIONS
WITH NOTES AND TABLATURE

Trans-Siberian Orchestra

GUITAR ANTHOLOGY

Cover photo by Bob Carey, courtesy of Trans-Siberian Orchestra

Music transcriptions by Addi Booth, Ron Piccione and David Stocker

ISBN 978-1-4950-3597-5

HAL•LEONARD®
CORPORATION

7777 W. BLUEMOUND RD. P.O. BOX 13819 MILWAUKEE, WI 53213

In Australia Contact:
Hal Leonard Australia Pty. Ltd.
4 Lentara Court
Cheltenham, Victoria, 3192 Australia
Email: ausadmin@halleonard.com.au

Visit Hal Leonard Online at
www.halleonard.com

Photo by Lewis Lee, courtesy of Trans-Siberian Orchestra

Beethoven

Music by Ludvig van Beethoven and W.A. Mozart
Arranged by Paul O'Neill and Robert Kinkel

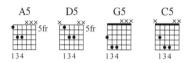

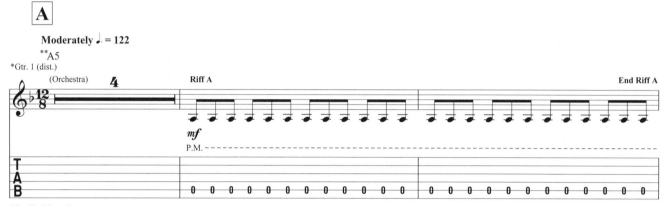

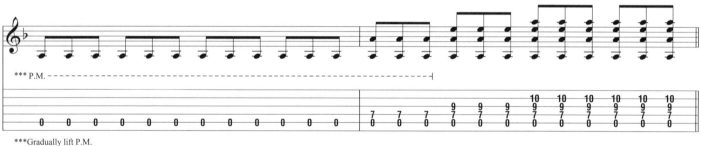

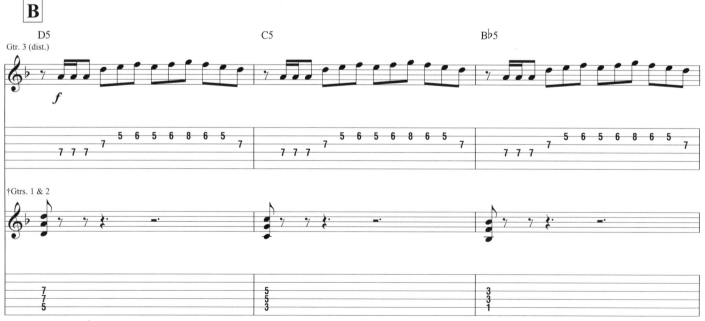

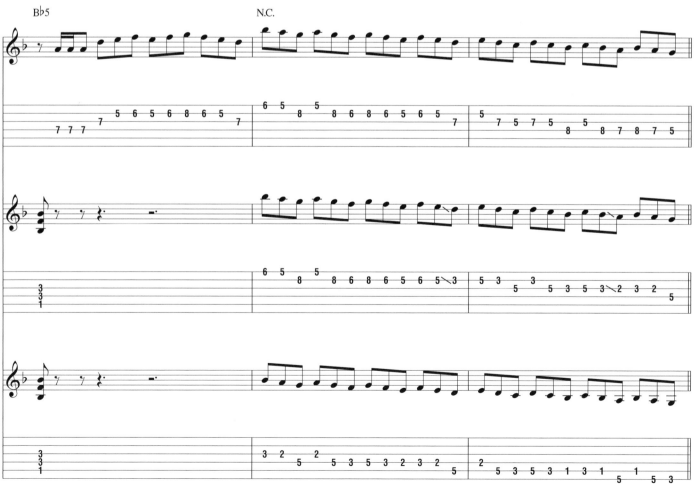

Gtr. 1: w/ Riff A (4 1/2 times)

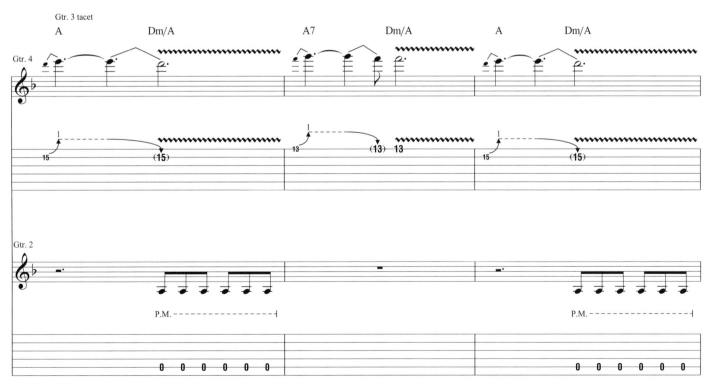

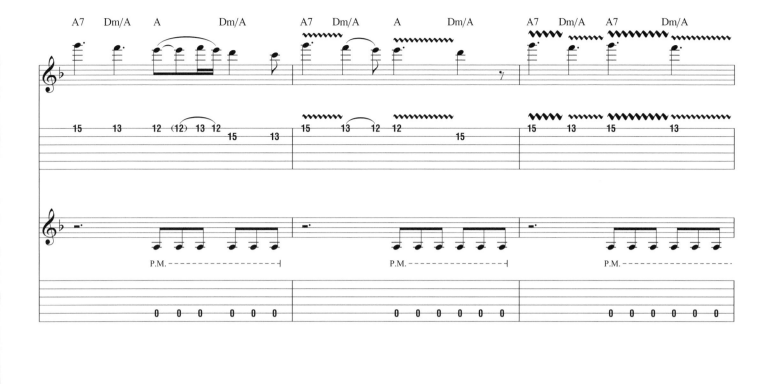

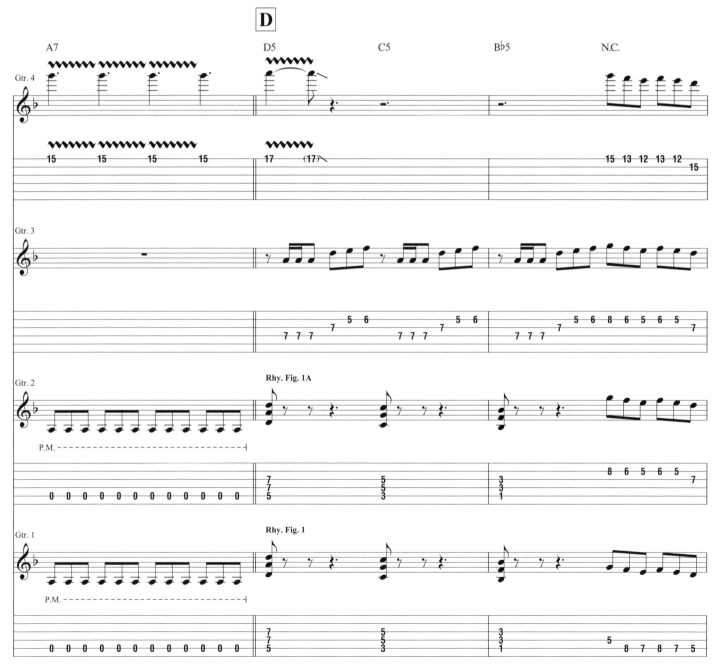

*See top of first page of song for chord diagrams pertaining to rhythm slashes.

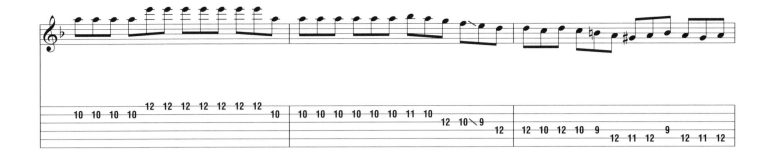

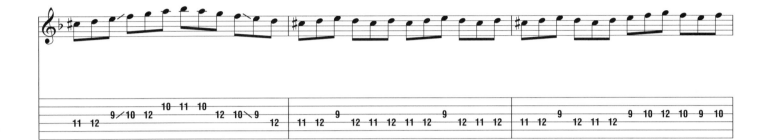

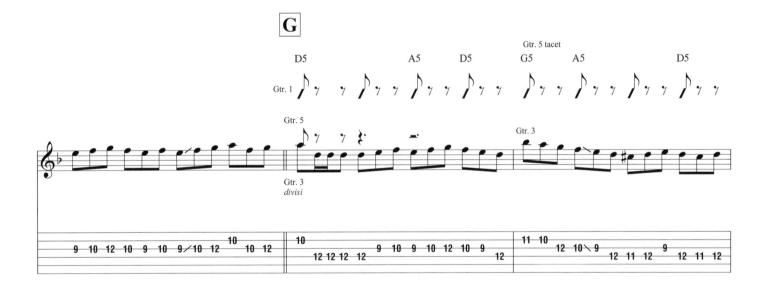

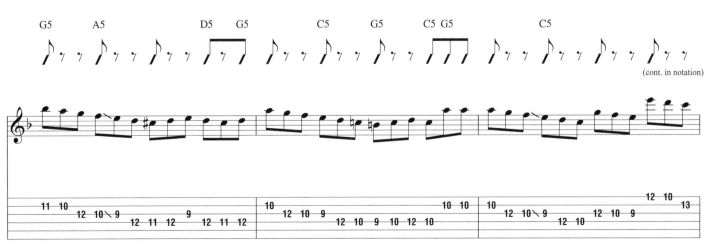

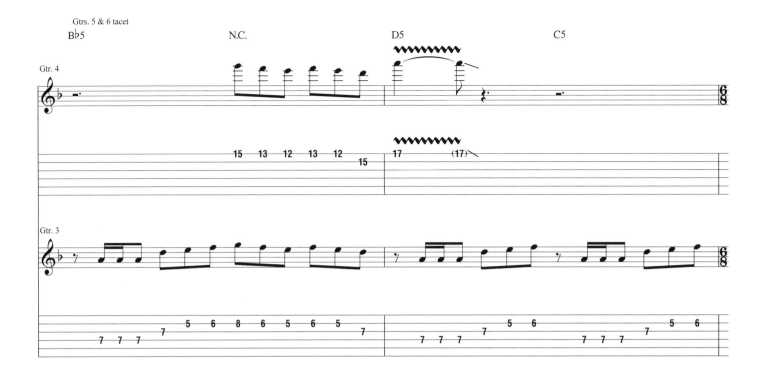

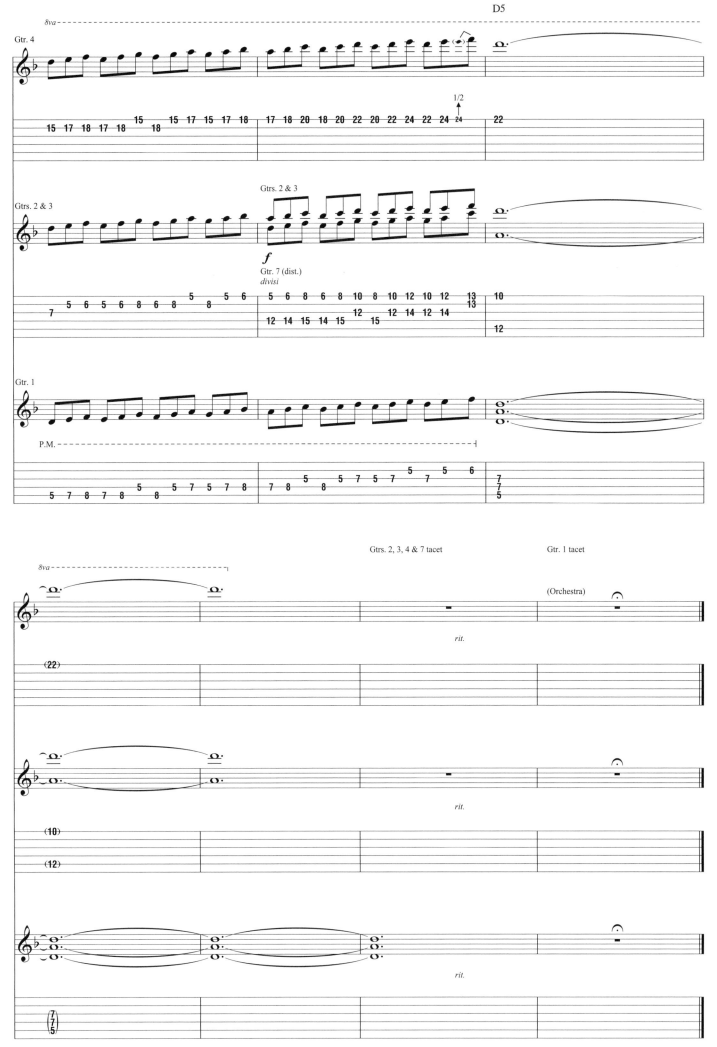

from Trans-Siberian Orchestra - *The Lost Christmas Eve*

Christmas Canon Rock

Music and Lyrics by Paul O'Neill

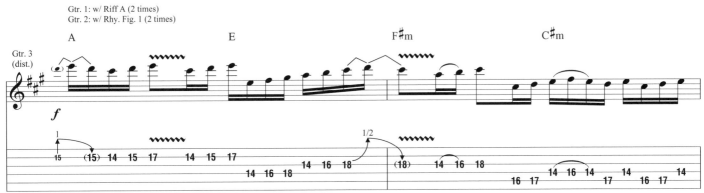

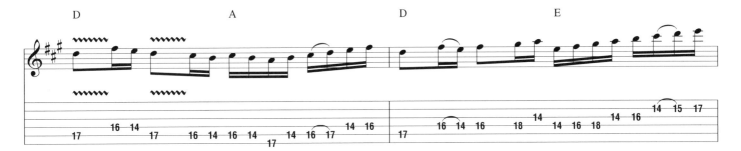

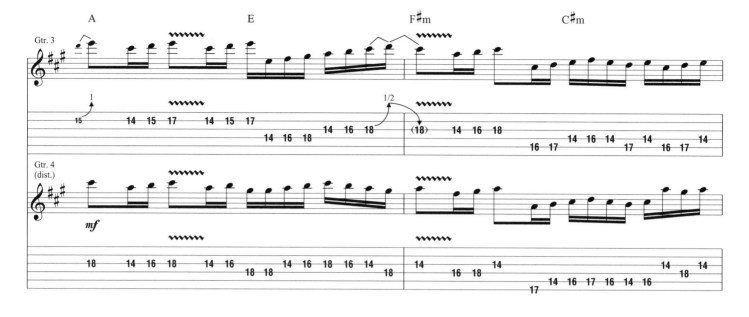

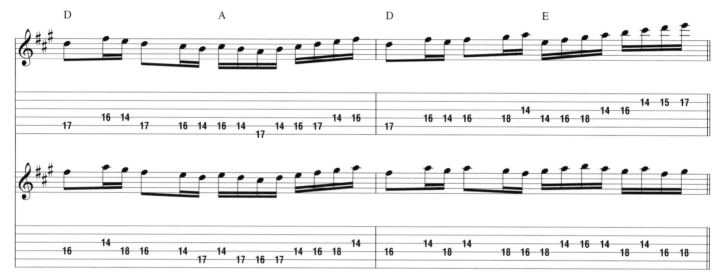

Verse

Gtr. 1: w/ Riff A (2 times)

Gtrs. 2, 3 & 4 tacet

1. *Fenale:* This night we pray. Our lives will show. This dream he had each child still knows.

*See top of first page of song for chord diagrams pertaining to rhythm slashes.

Guitar Solo

Gtr. 1: w/ Riff A (2 times)
Gtr. 2: w/ Rhy. Fig. 1 (2 times)

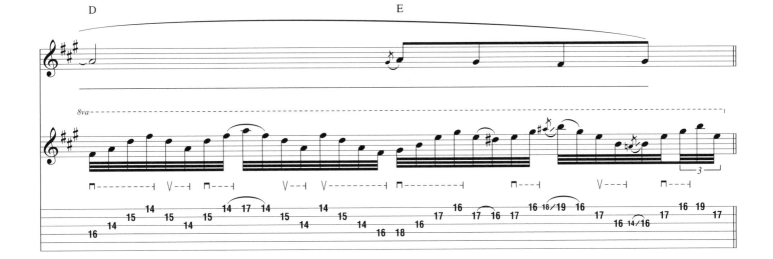

Outro

Gtr. 1: w/ Riff A (1 1/2 times)
Gtr. 2: w/ Rhy. Fig. 1 (1 1/2 times)

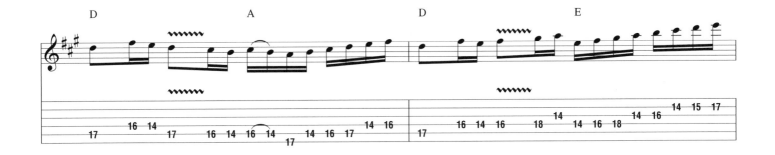

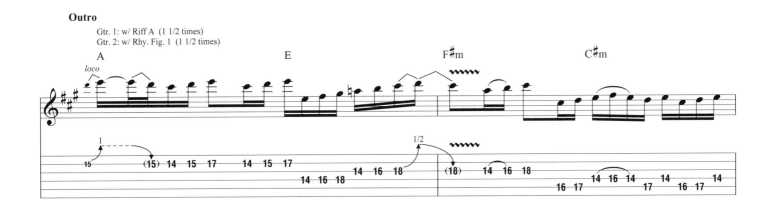

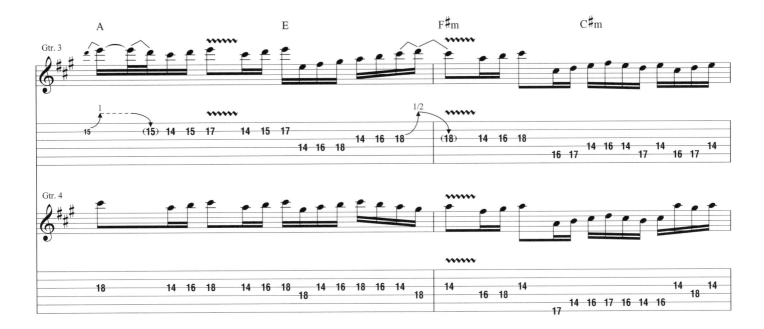

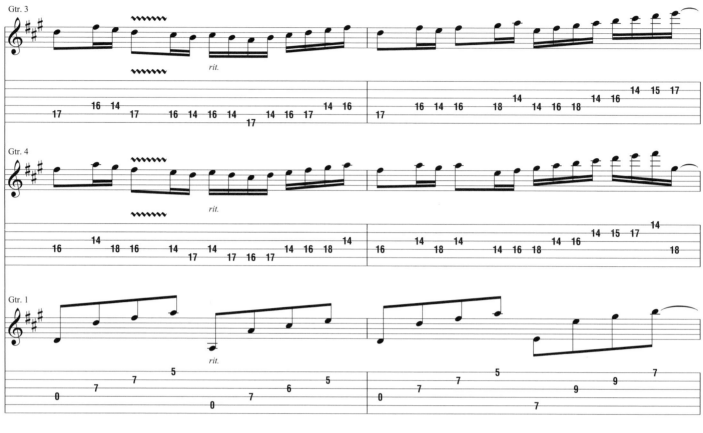

Free time

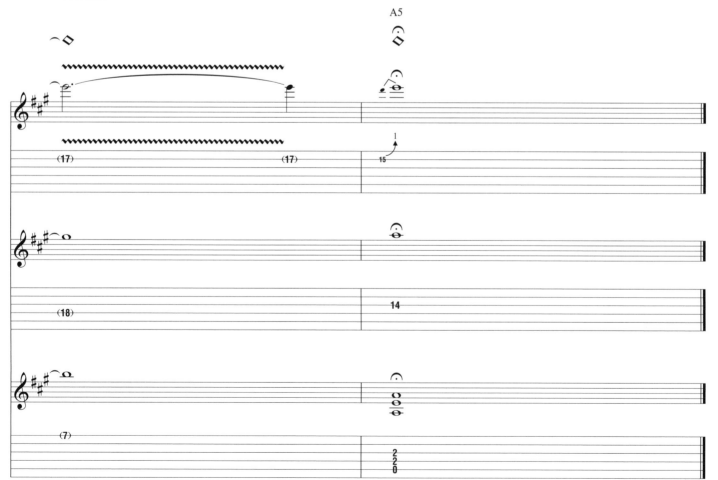

Christmas Eve/Sarajevo 12/24

Music by Paul O'Neill and Robert Kinkel

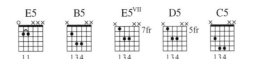

Gtr. 1 tuning:
(low to high) E-A-D-G-B-F♯

*Cello arr. for gtr.

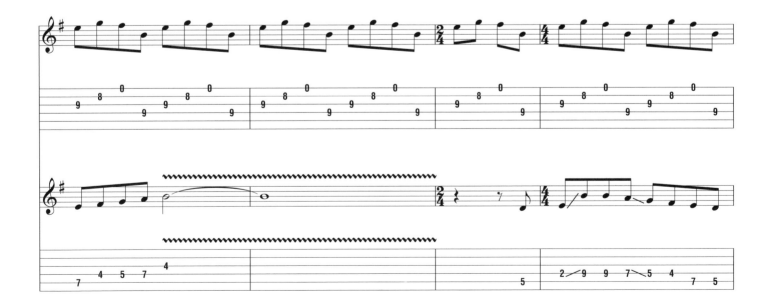

B

Very fast ♩ = 180

Gtrs. 1 & 2 tacet

**E5

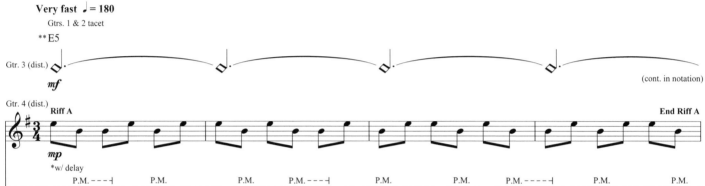

(cont. in notation)

Gtr. 4 (dist.)

Riff A

End Riff A

*w/ delay

*Set for dotted-eighth-note regeneration w/ 1 repeat.

**See top of first page of song for chord diagrams pertaining to rhythm slashes.

Gtr. 4: w/ Riff A (5 times)

E5

Gtr. 3

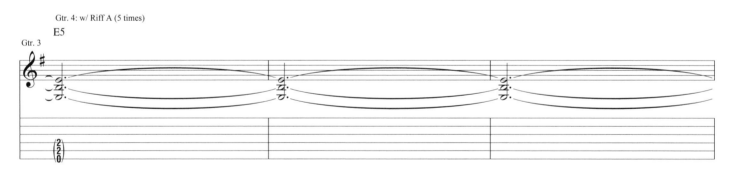

**Gtr. 5

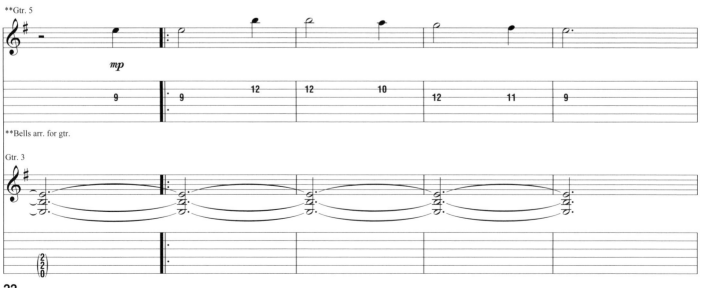

**Bells arr. for gtr.

Gtr. 3

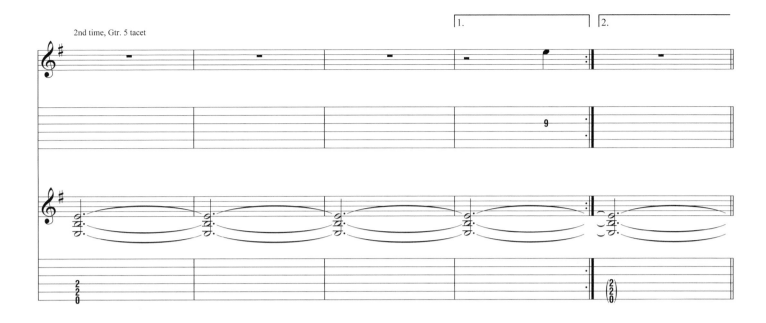

2nd time, Gtr. 5 tacet

C

Gtr. 4: w/ Riff A (3 times)

*Em

Riff B   End Riff B

Gtr. 6 (dist.)

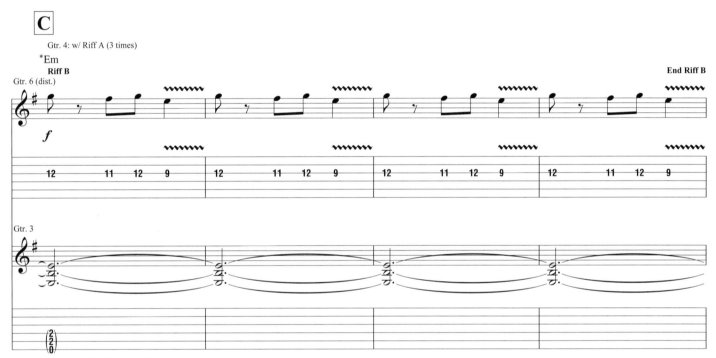

*Chord symbols reflect overall harmony.

Gtr. 6: w/ Riff B

Riff C   End Riff C

Gtr. 7 (dist.)

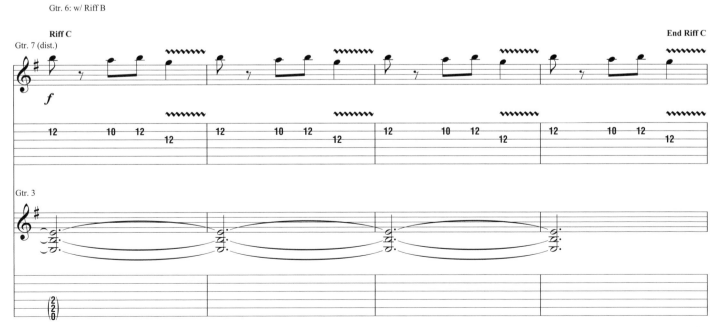

Gtr. 4: w/ Riff E

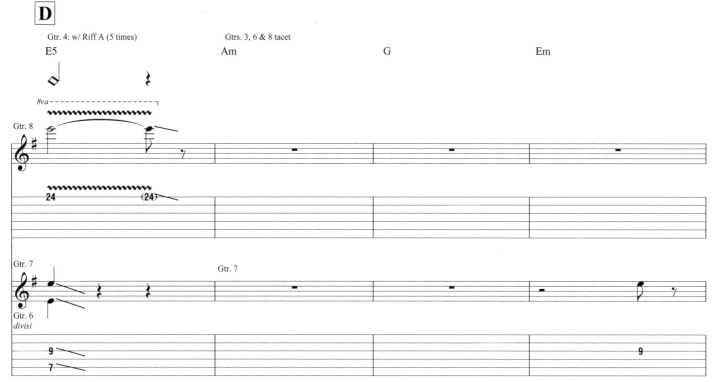

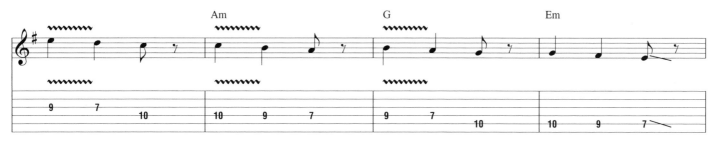

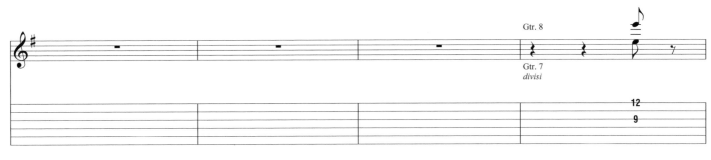

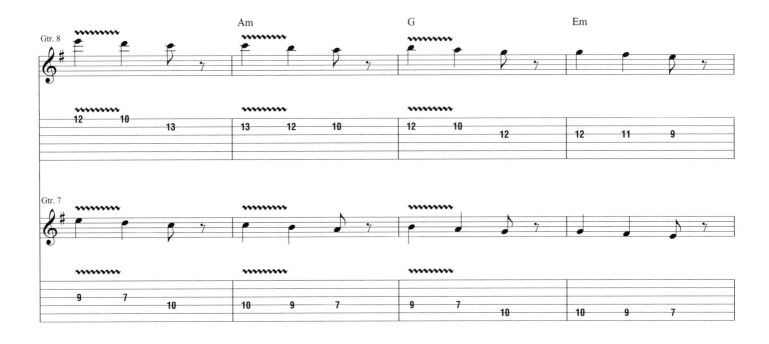

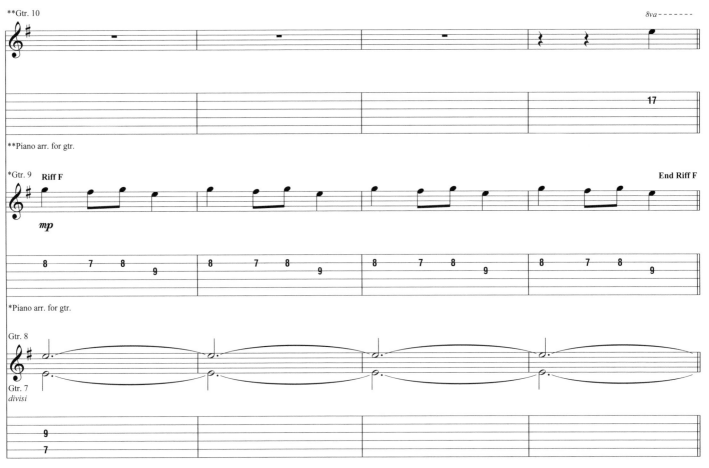

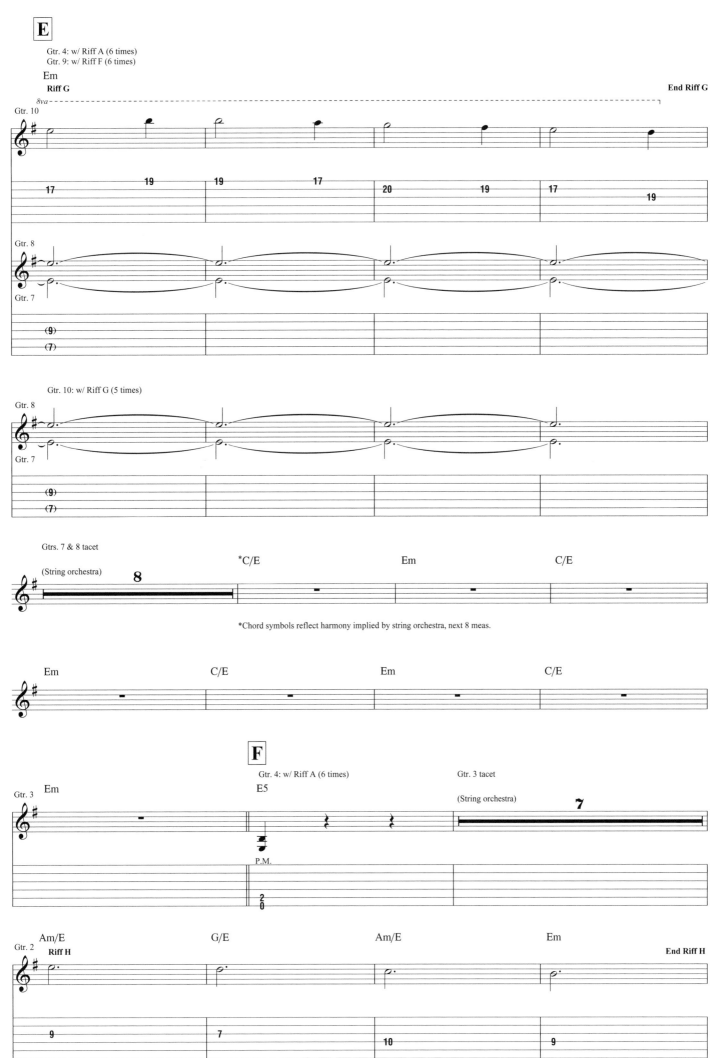

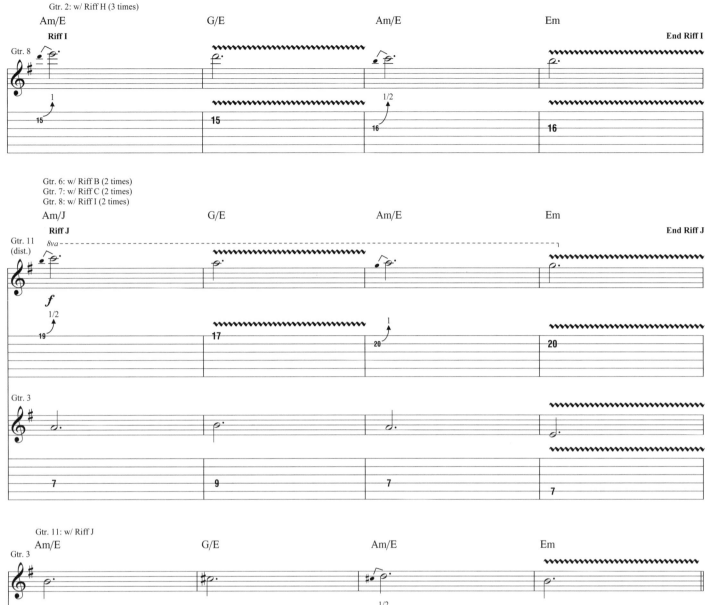

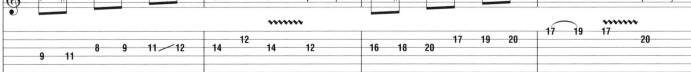

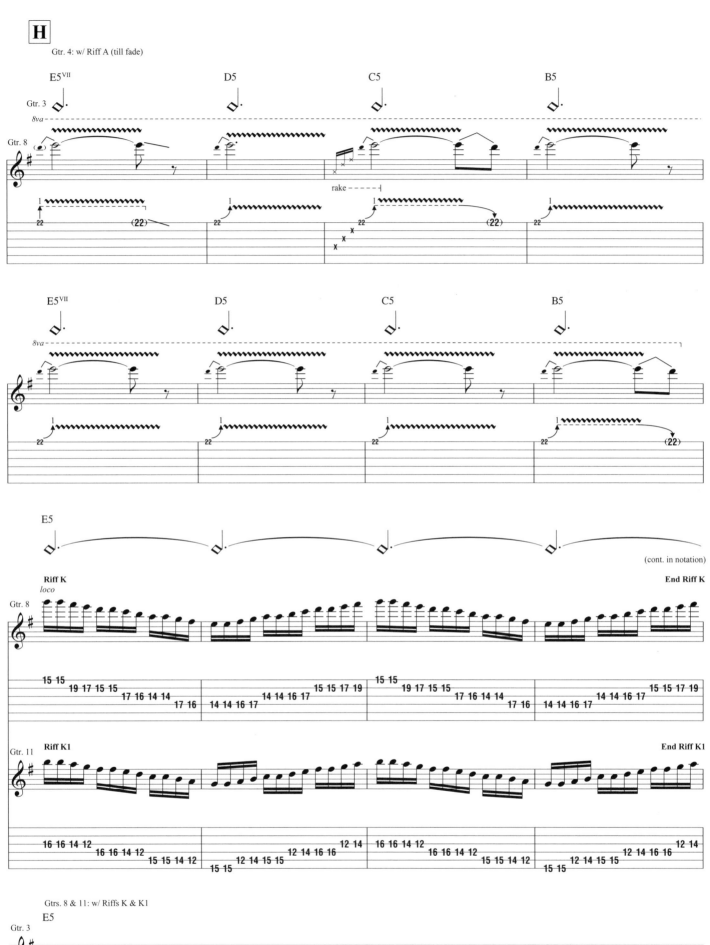

Play 3 times and fade

Gtrs. 3, 8 & 11 tacet

Dreams of Fireflies

Music by Paul O'Neill

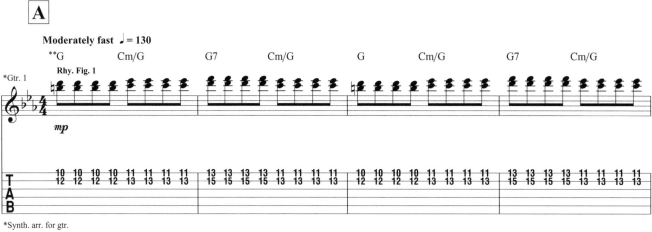

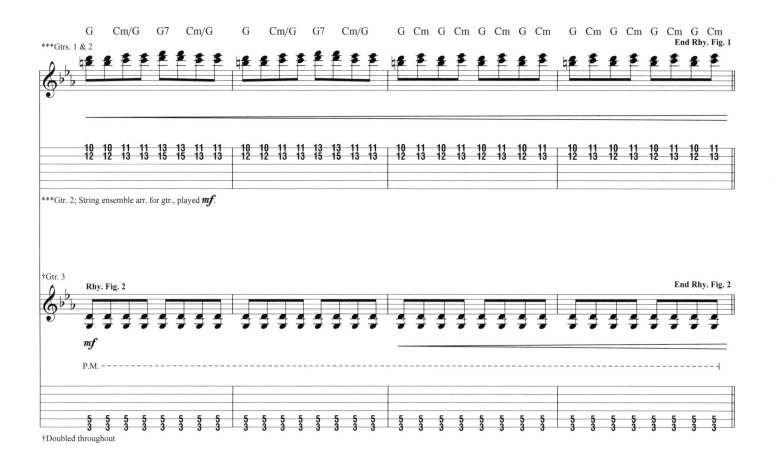

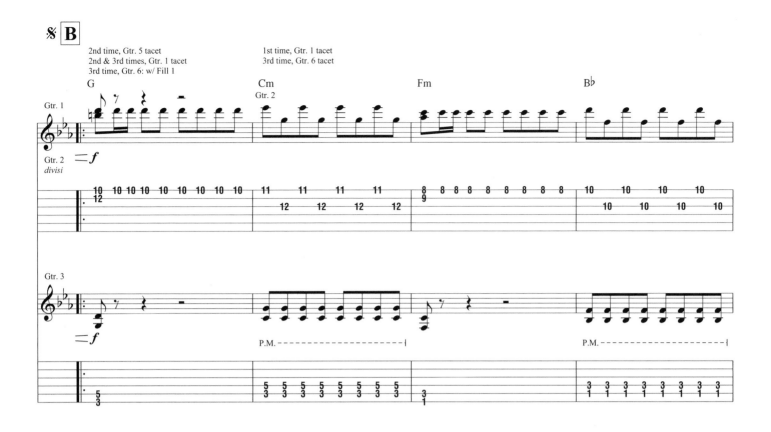

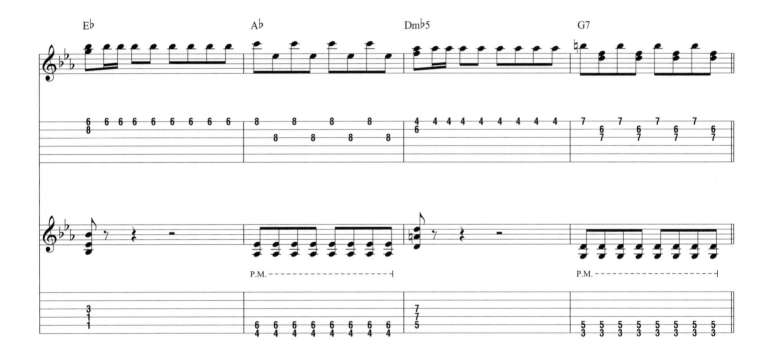

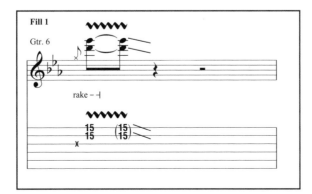

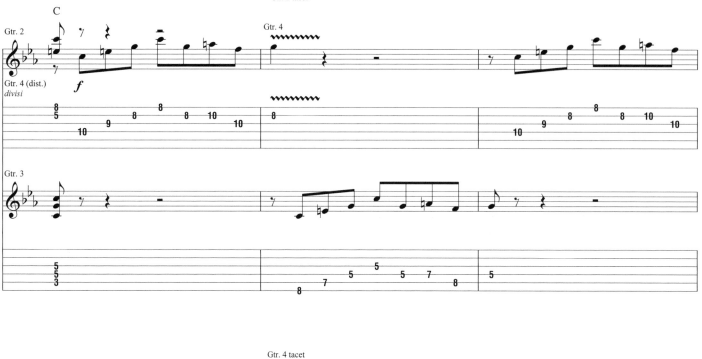

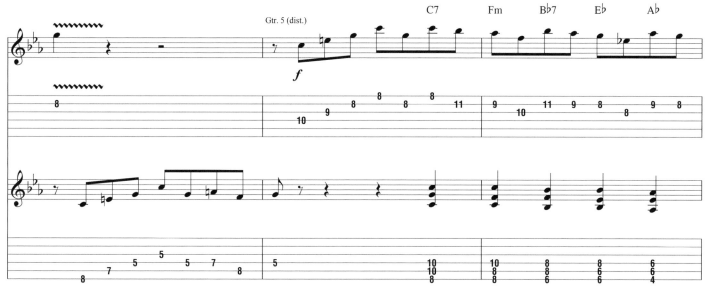

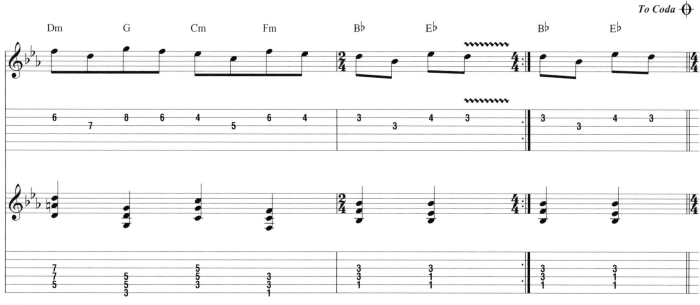

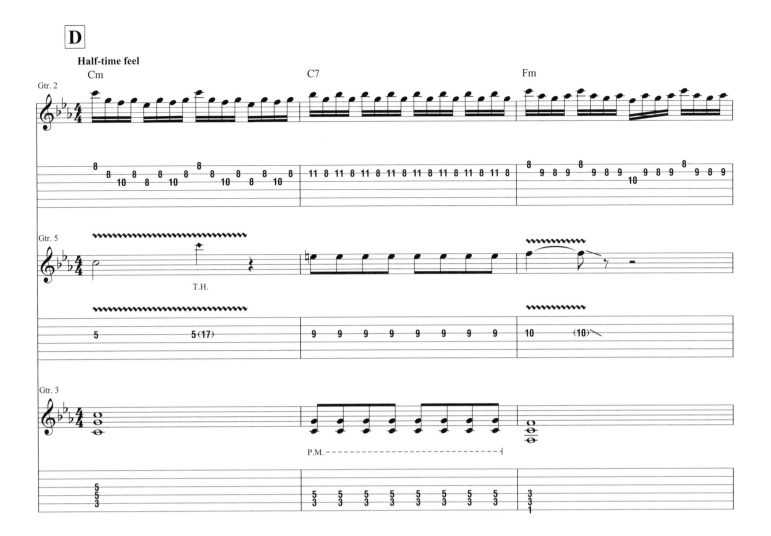

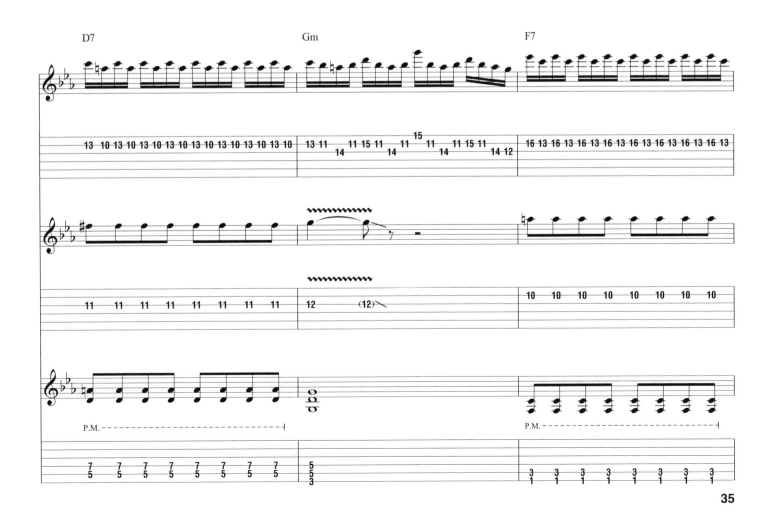

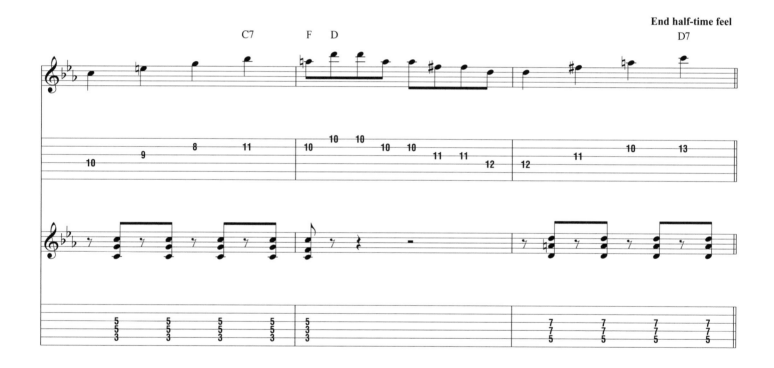

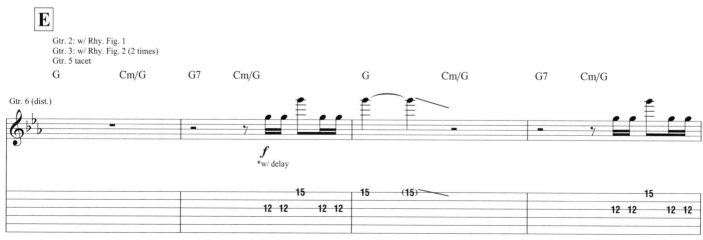

*Set for quarter-note regeneration w/ 1 repeat.

First Snow

Music by Paul O'Neill

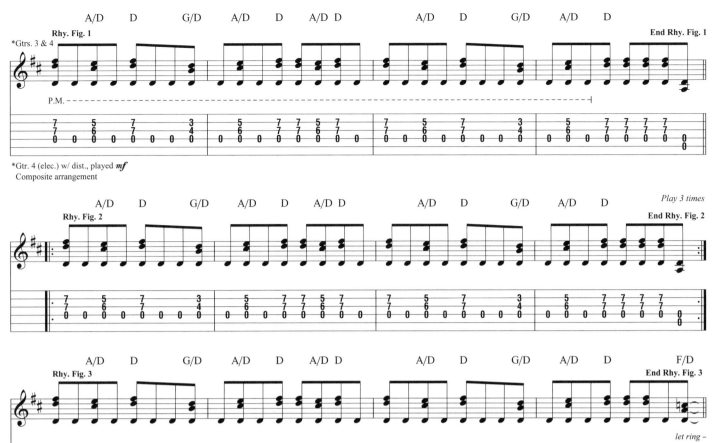

*Gtr. 4 (elec.) w/ dist., played **mf***
Composite arrangement

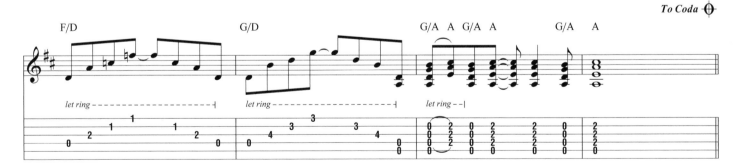

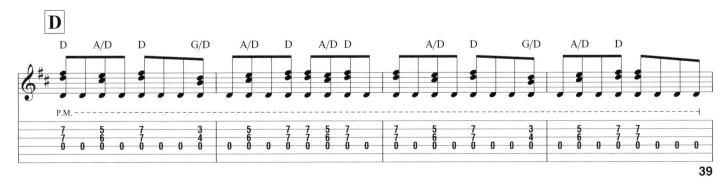

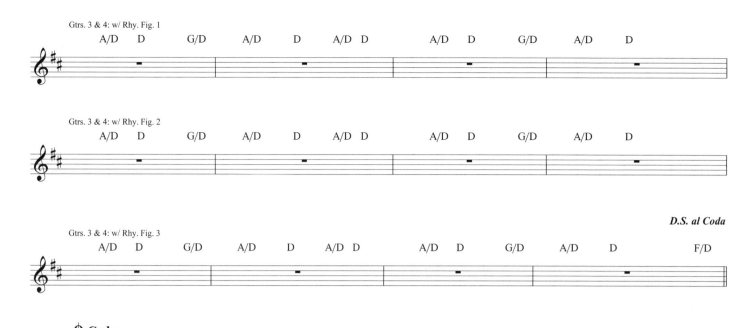

D.S. al Coda

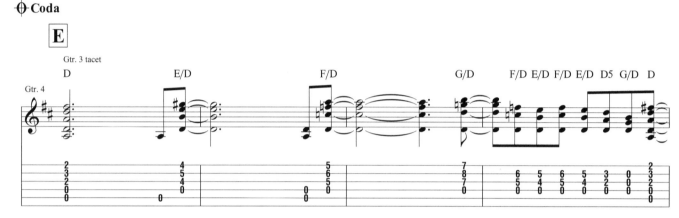

⊕ Coda

E

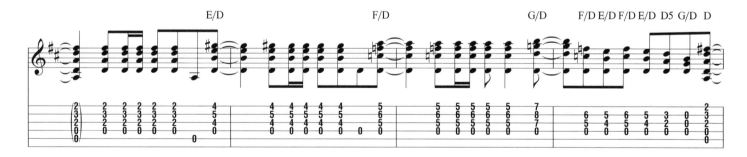

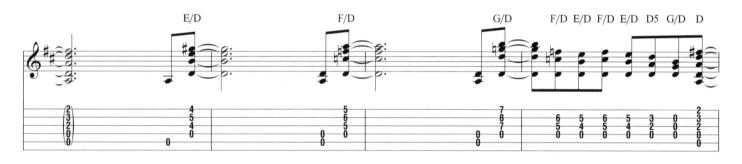

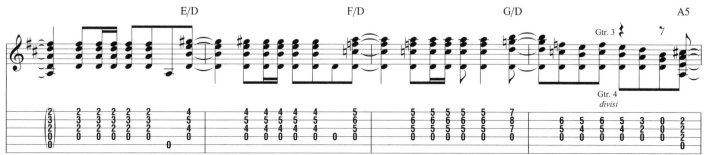

A Mad Russian's Christmas

Music by Paul O'Neill, Robert Kinkel and Peter Ilyich Tchaikovsky

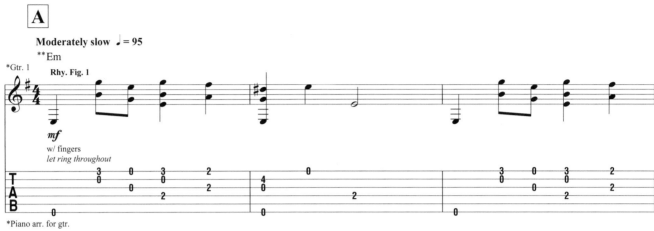

*Piano arr. for gtr.

**Chord symbols reflect overall harmony.

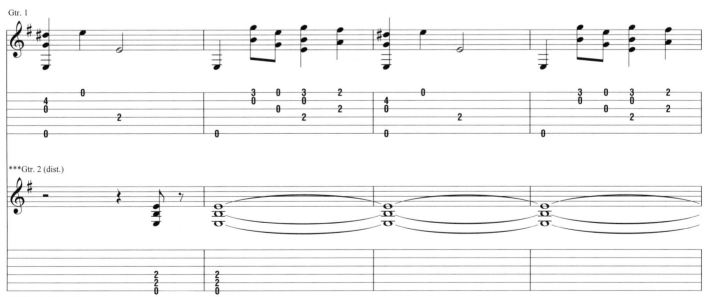

***Doubled throughout

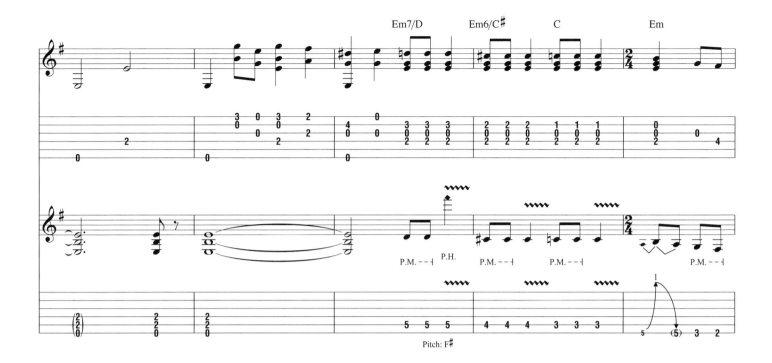

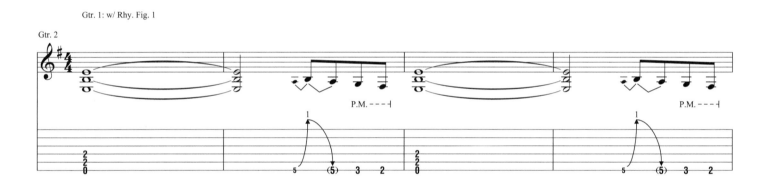

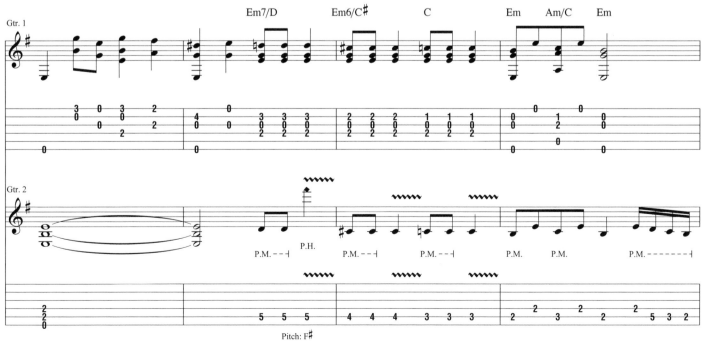

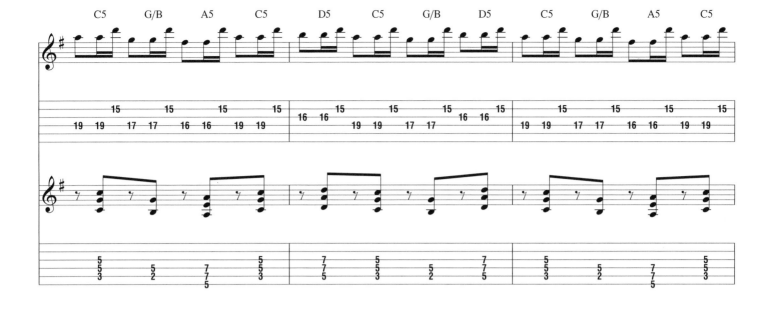

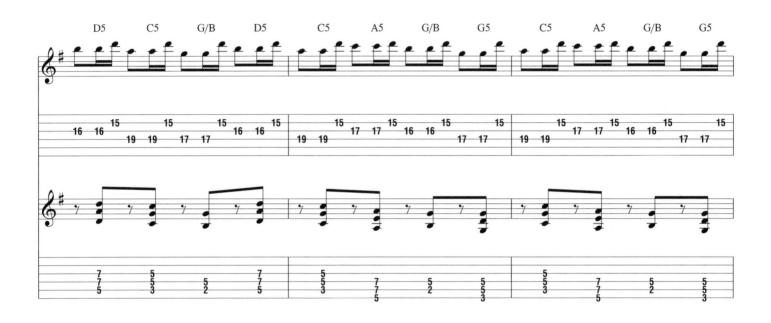

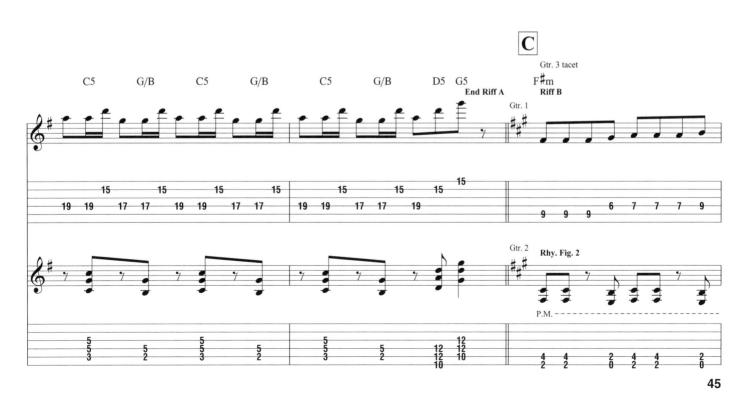

E

Gtrs. 1 & 3: w/ Riff B
Gtr. 2: w/ Rhy. Fig. 2 (5 times)
Gtr. 6 tacet

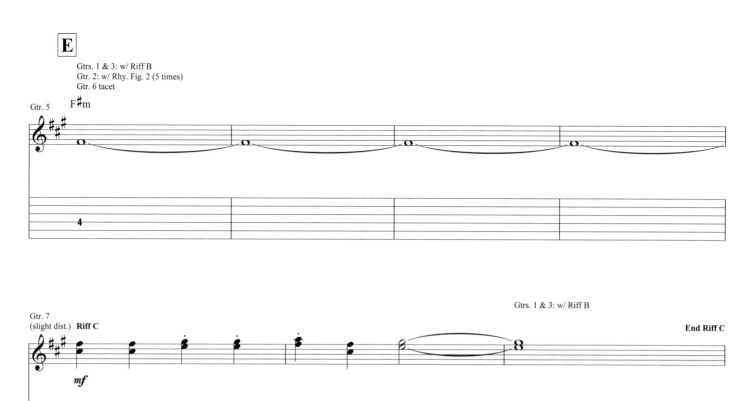

Gtr. 7
(slight dist.) **Riff C**

Gtrs. 1 & 3: w/ Riff B

End Riff C

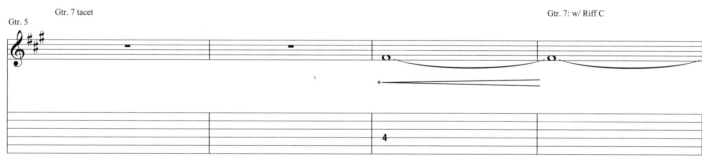

Gtr. 5

Gtr. 7 tacet

Gtr. 7: w/ Riff C

*Vol. swells

Gtrs. 1 & 3: w/ Riff B

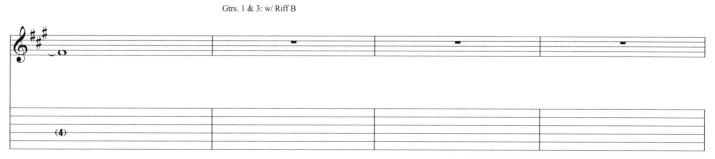

Gtr. 7: w/ Riff C

Gtrs. 1 & 3: w/ Riff B

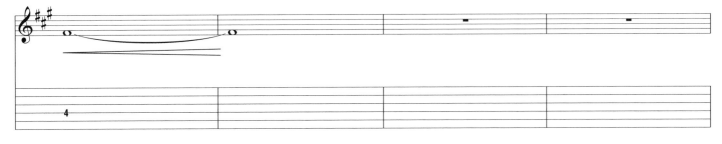

Gtr. 2: w/ Rhy. Fig. 3

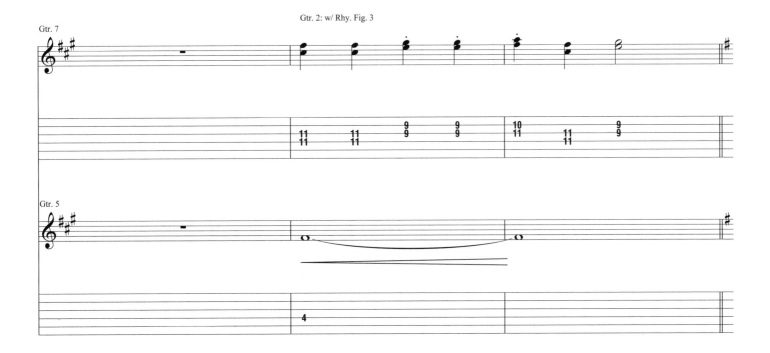

F

Gtrs. 5 & 7 tacet

G

Gtr. 1   **Rhy. Fig. 4**

End Rhy. Fig. 4

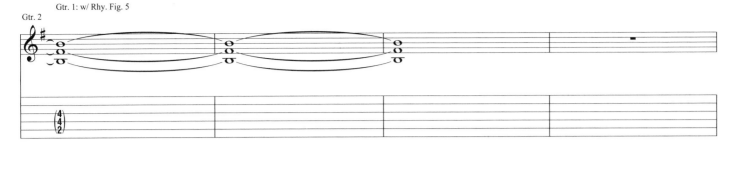

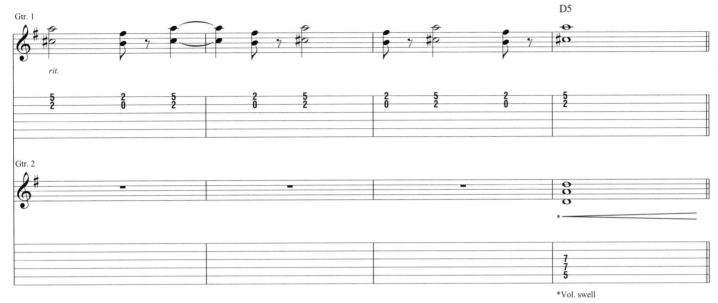

*Vol. swell

H

A tempo
Gtr. 1 tacet
Gtr. 3: w/ Riff A (1st 6 meas.)

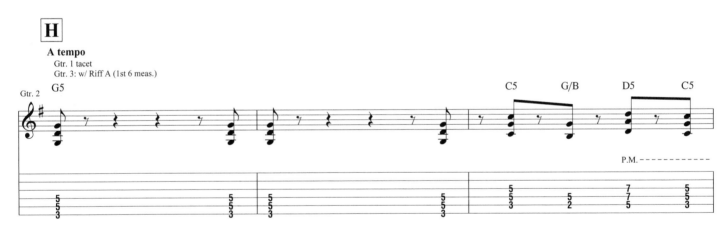

54

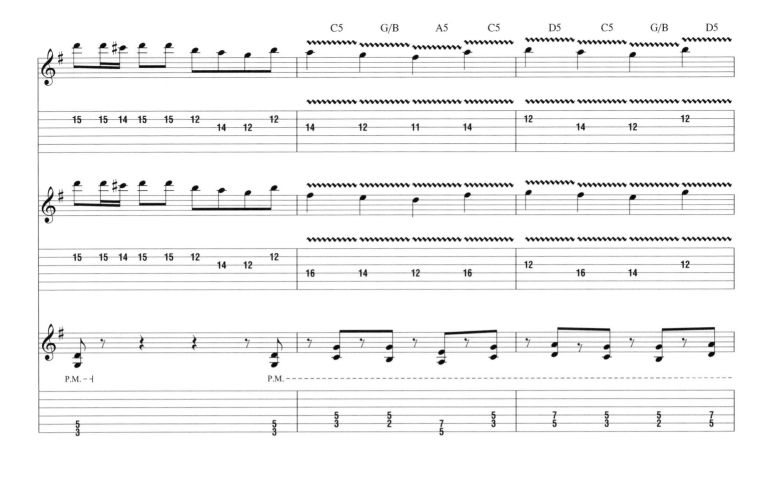

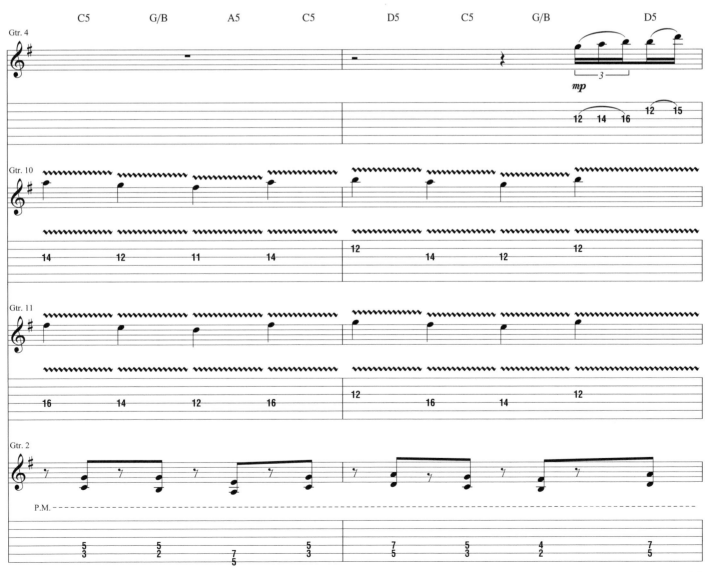

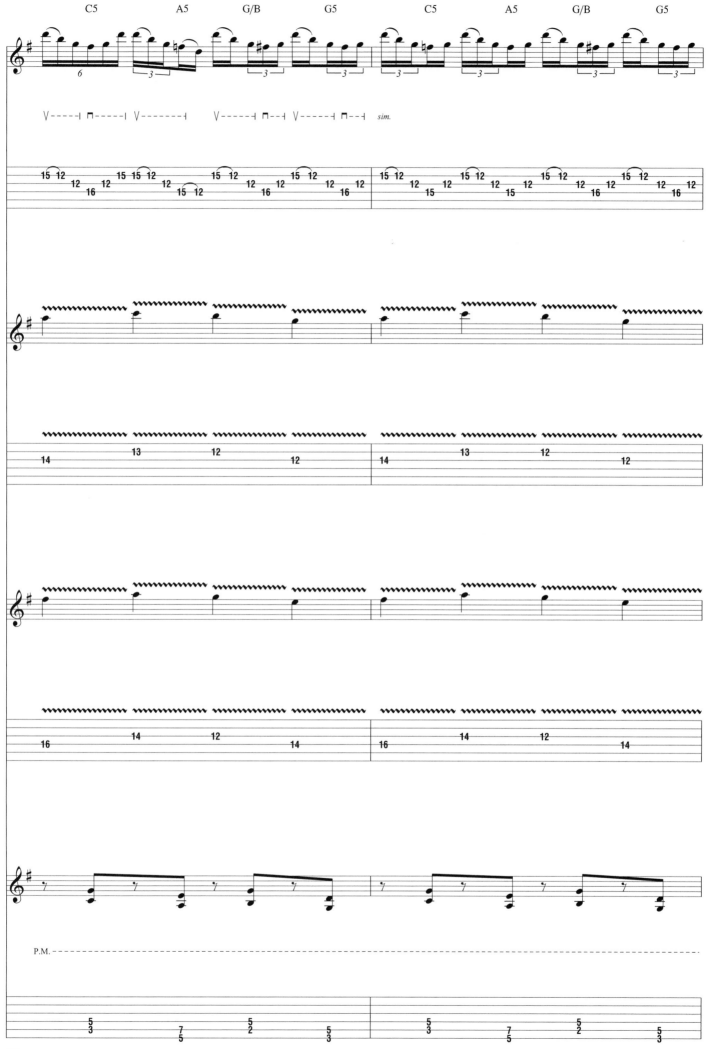

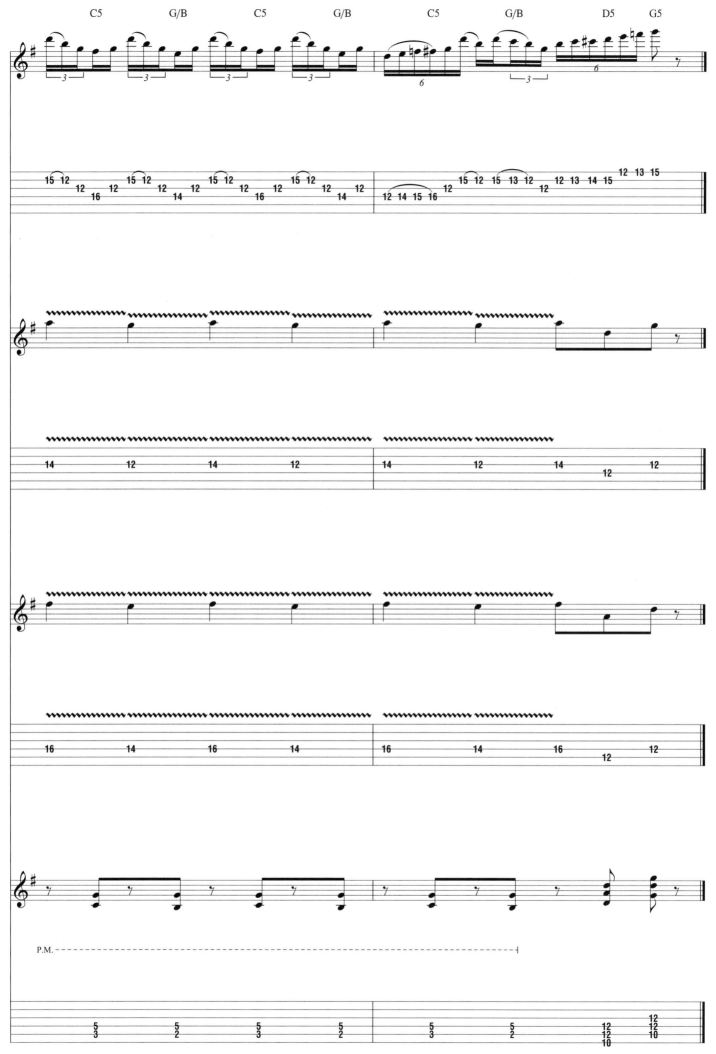

from Trans-Siberian Orchestra - *Night Castle*
The Mountain
Based upon MARS, THE BRINGER OF WAR from THE PLANETS by Gustav Holst
and IN THE HALL OF THE MOUNTAIN KING by Edvard Greig
Arrangement and Additional Music by Paul O'Neill and John Oliva

*Strings arr. for gtr.

**Chord symbols reflect implied harmony.

***Doubled throughout

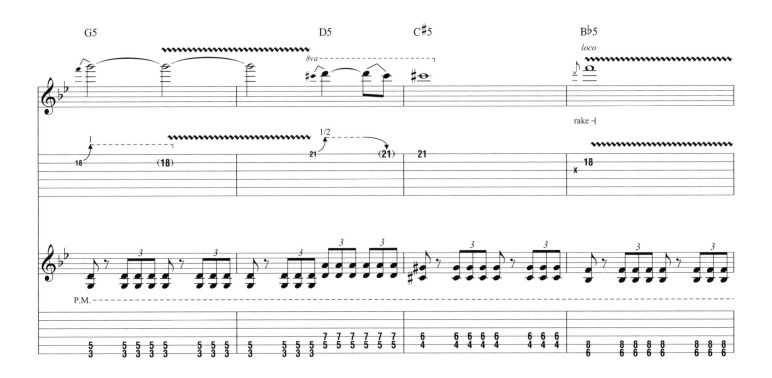

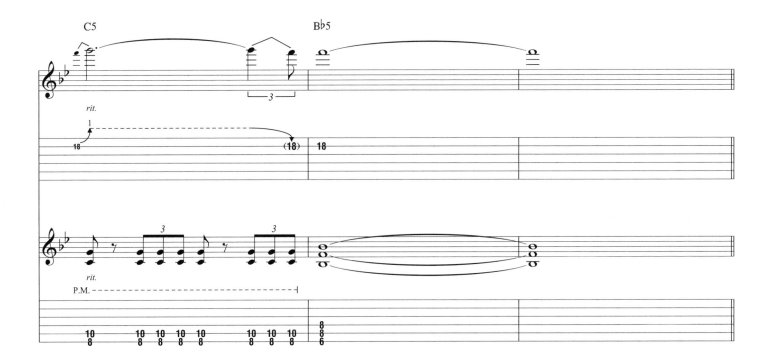

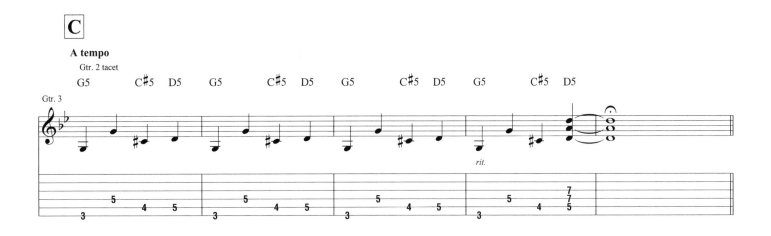

D

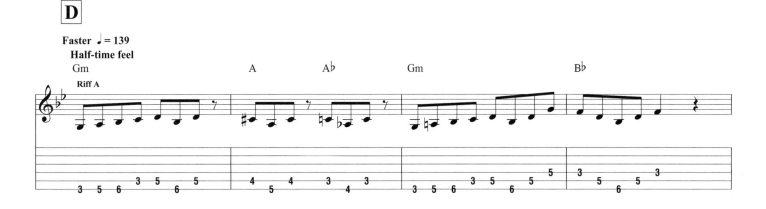

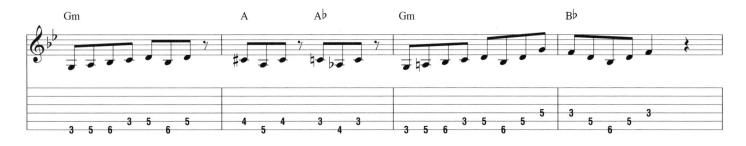

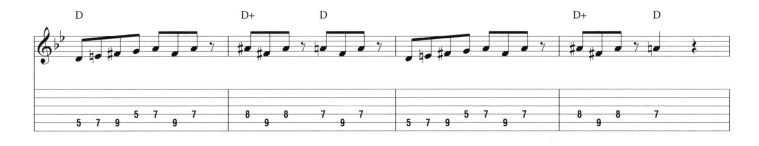

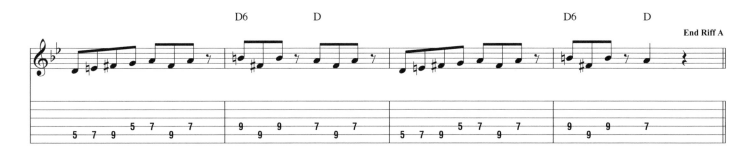

E

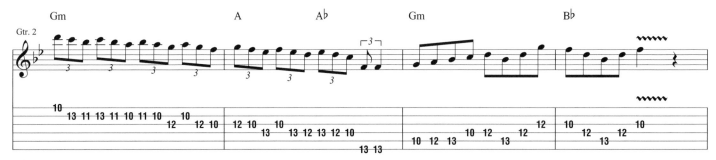

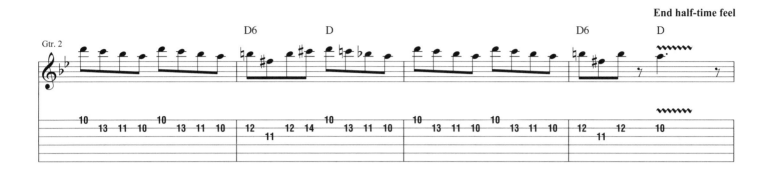

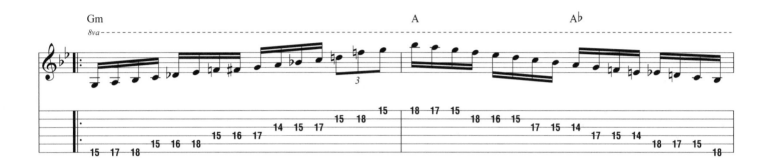

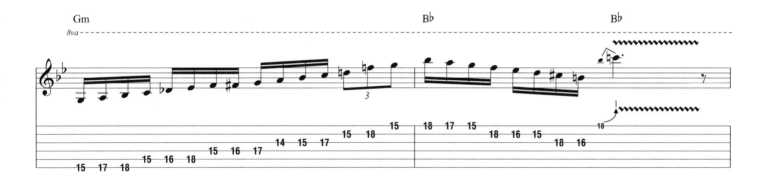

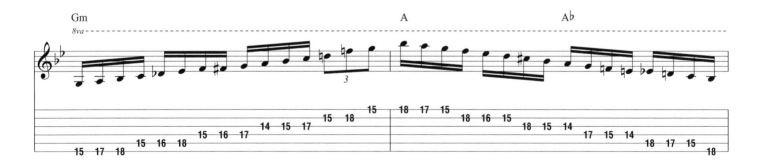

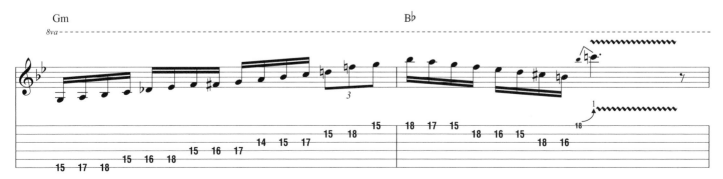

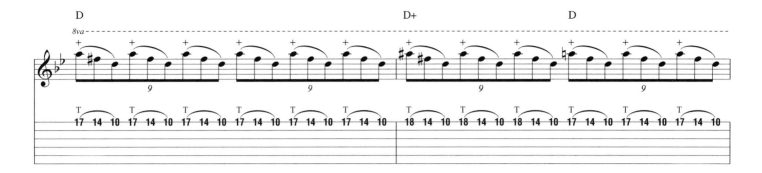

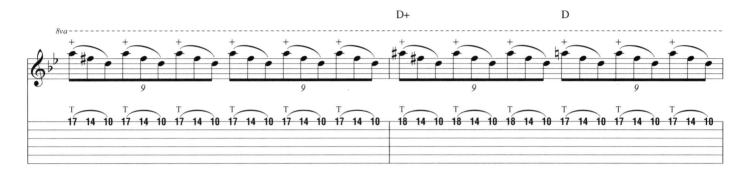

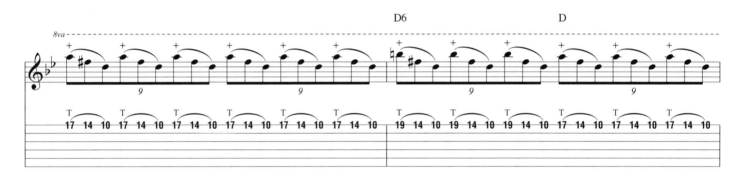

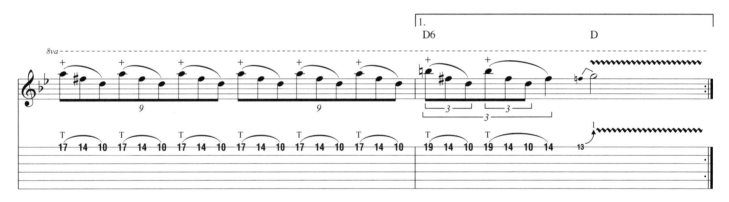

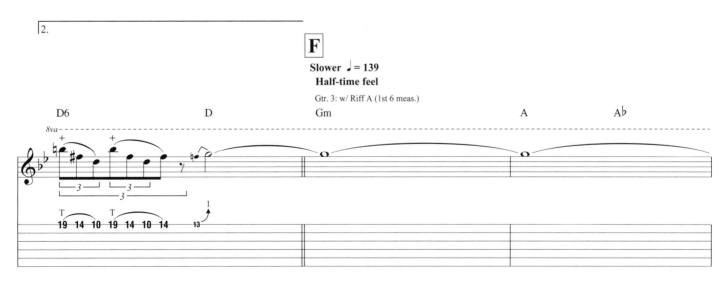

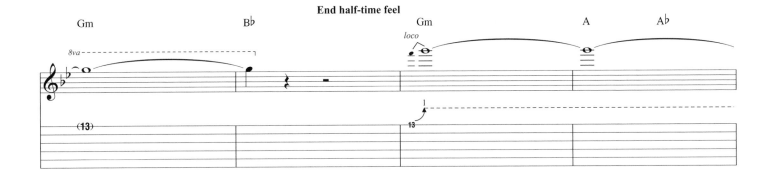

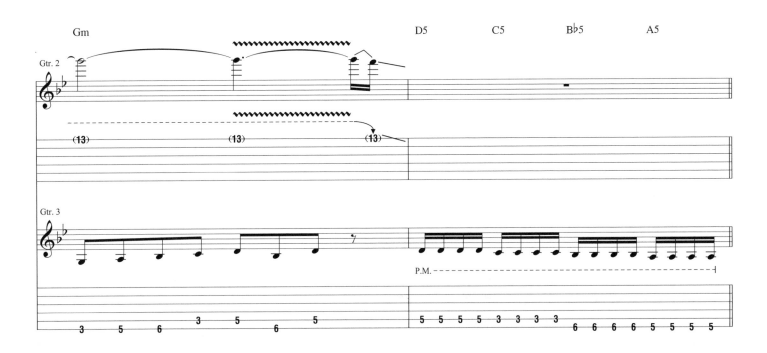

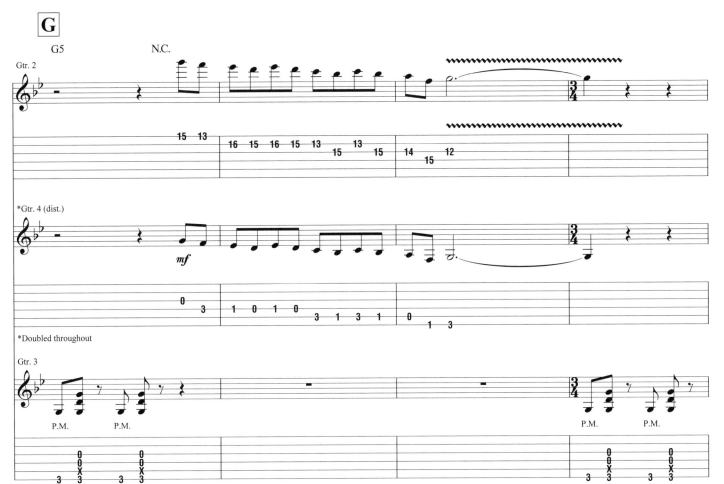

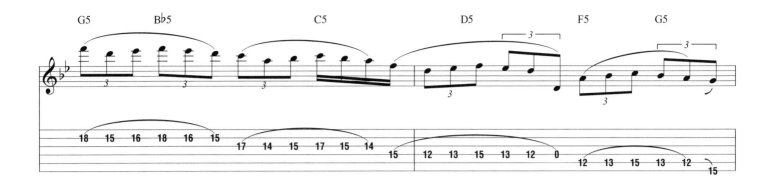

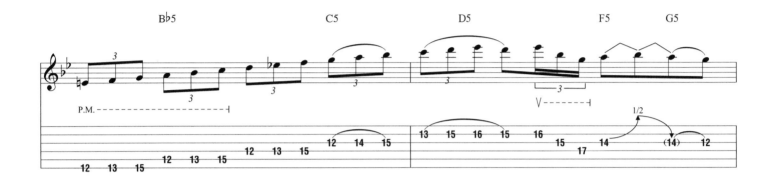

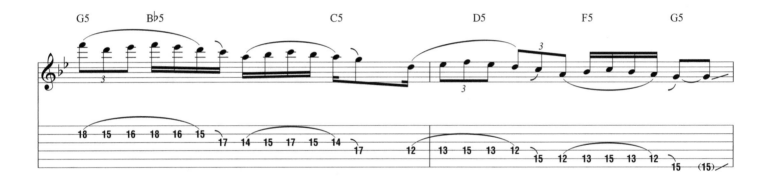

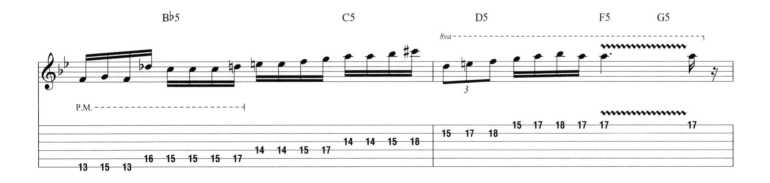

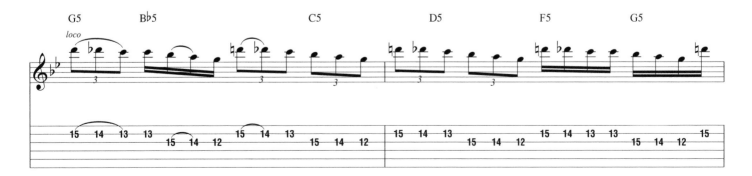

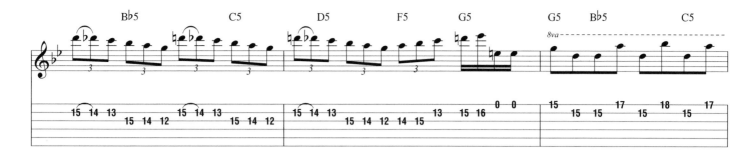

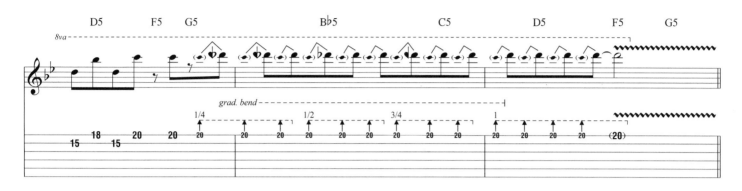

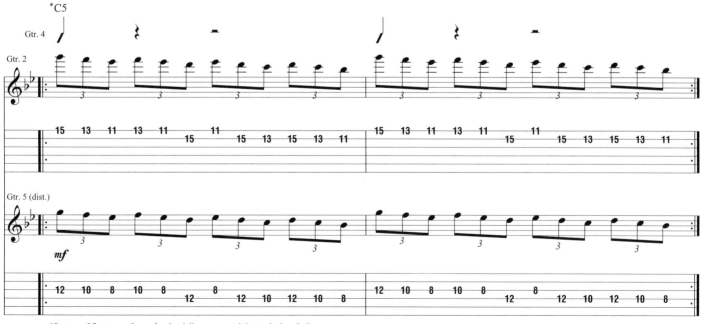

*See top of first page of song for chord diagrams pertaining to rhythm slashes.

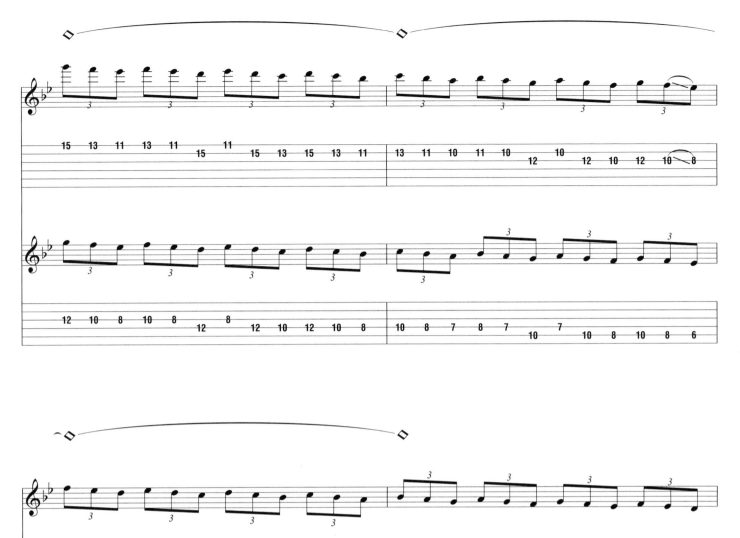

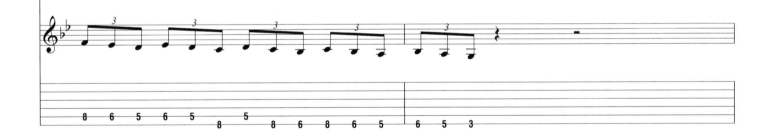

Gtr. 5 tacet

G5

Gtr. 2

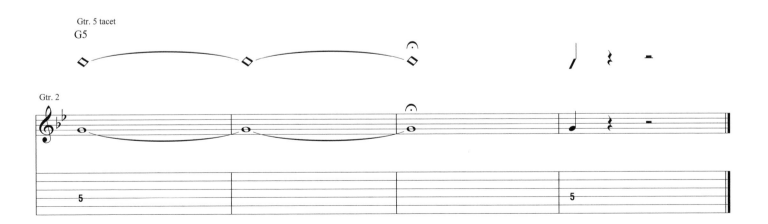

from Savatage - *Dead Winter Dead*
Mozart and Madness

Music by Paul O'Neill and John Oliva

Gtr. 5: Drop D tuning:
(low to high) D-A-D-G-B-E

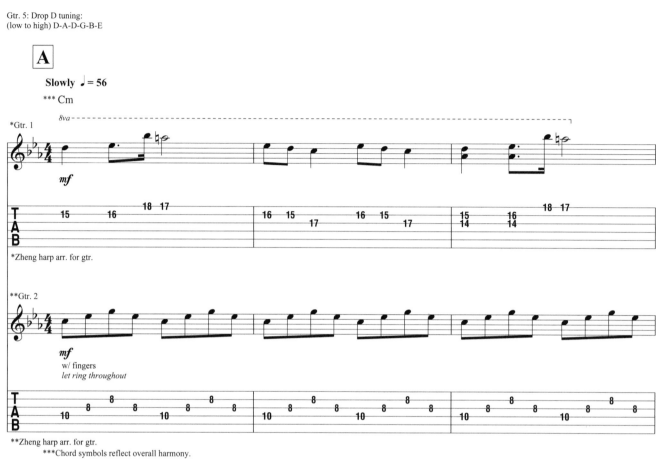

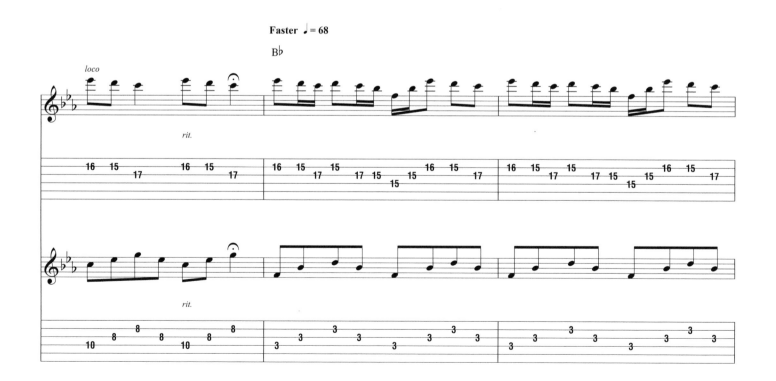

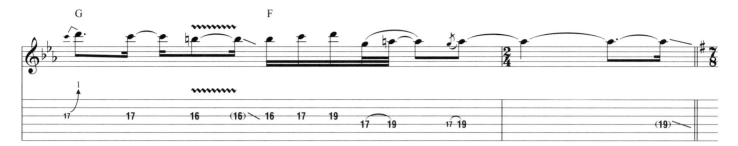

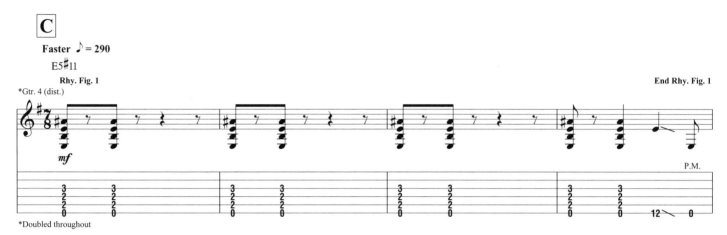

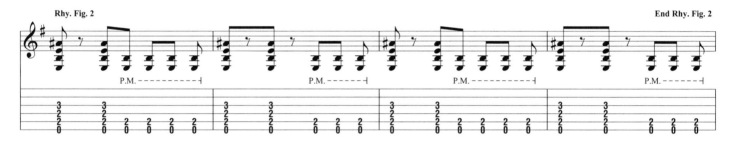

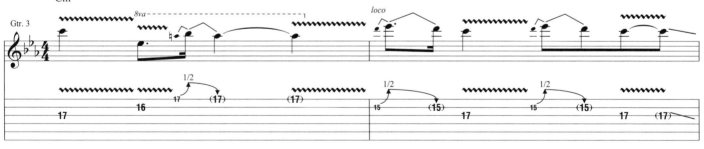

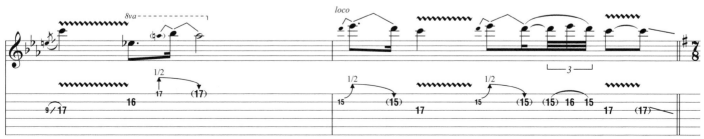

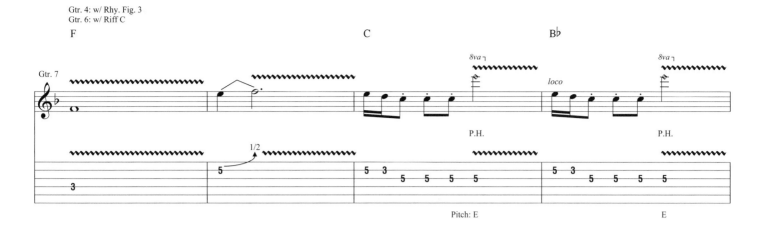

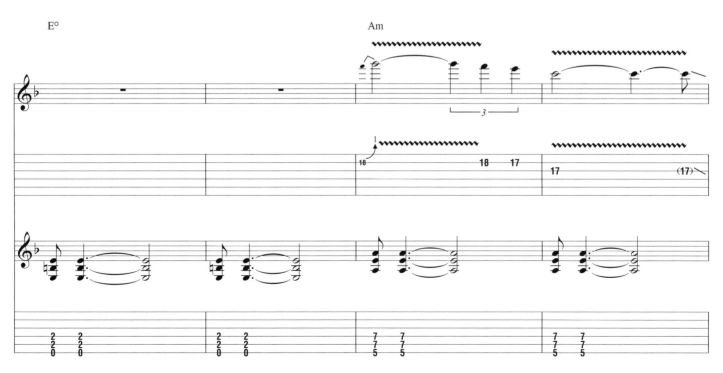

74

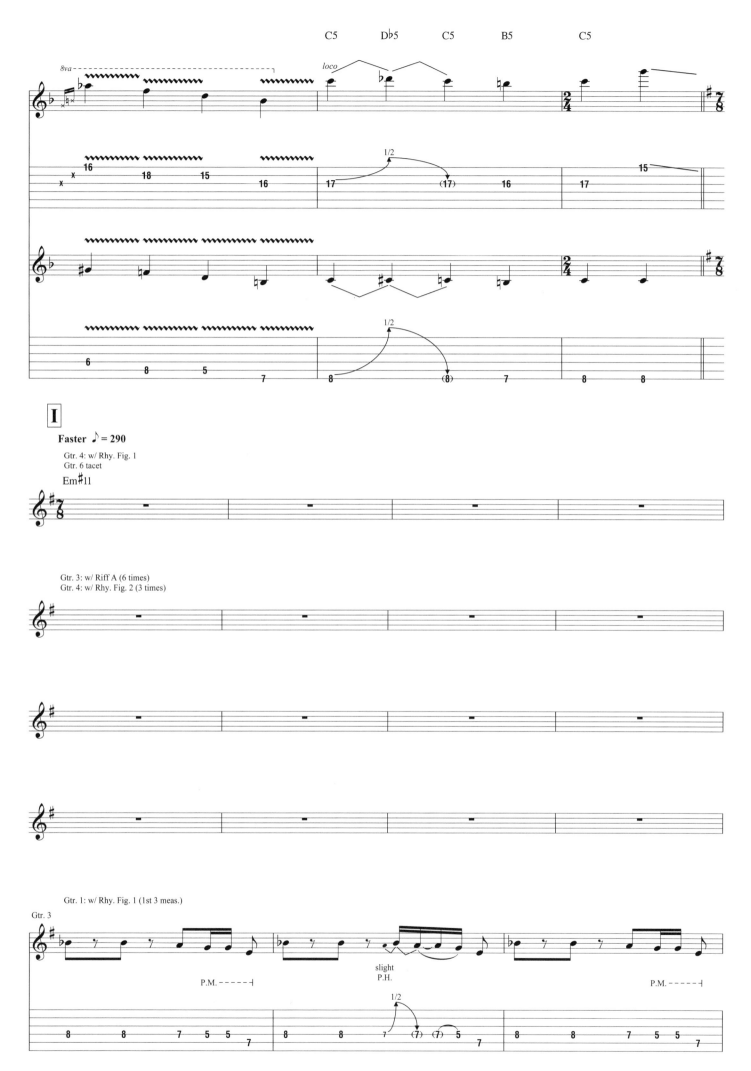

J

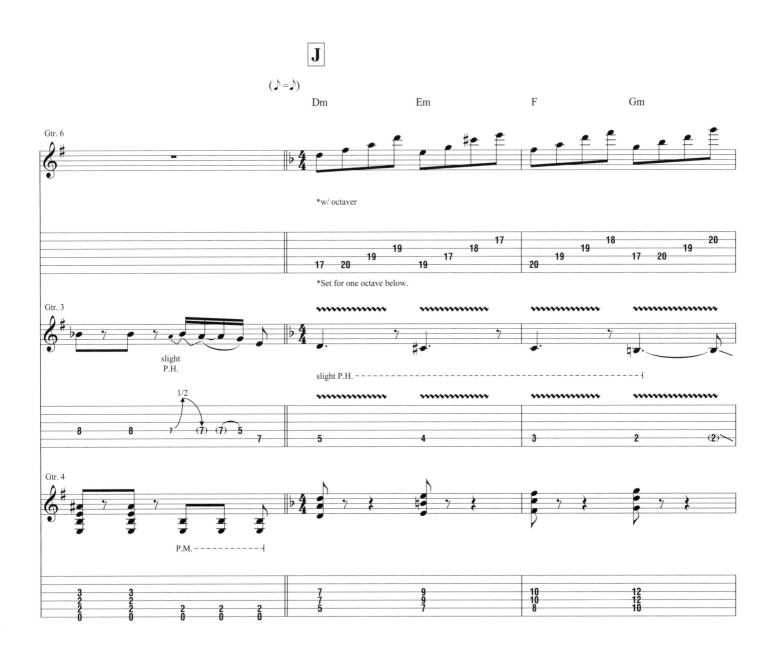

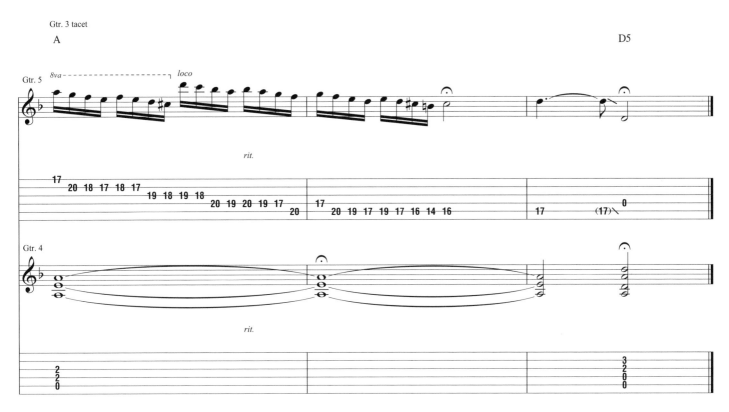

Old City Bar

Music and Lyrics by Paul O'Neill

Tune down 1 step:
(low to high) D-G-C-F-A-D

Gtrs. 2 & 3: Capo III

*Symbols in parentheses represent chord names respective to capoed guitar.
Symbols above reflect actual sounding chords. Capoed fret is "0" in tab.
Chord symbols reflect overall harmony.

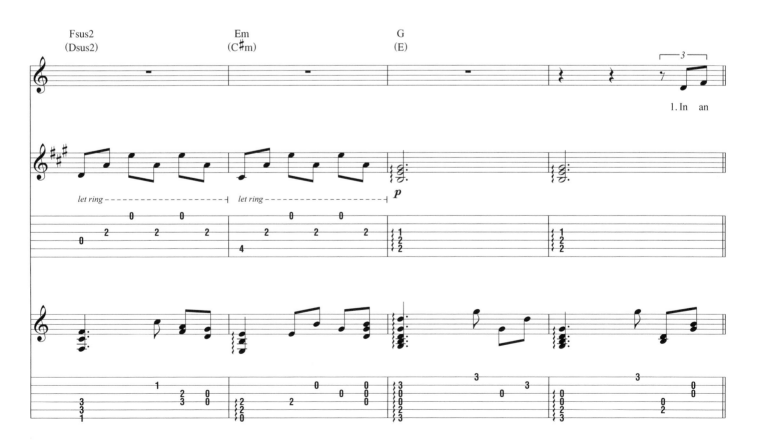

1. In an

Verse

old cit - y bar ___ that's nev - er too far ___ from the

plac - es that gath - er the dreams that have been. In the

safe - ty of night with it's old ne - on ___ light, it

A tempo

here was the dang - er   e - ven   with strang - ers,   in -

side   of   this   night ___   it's   eas - i - er ___   to   be - lieve.

End Rhy. Fig. 2

83

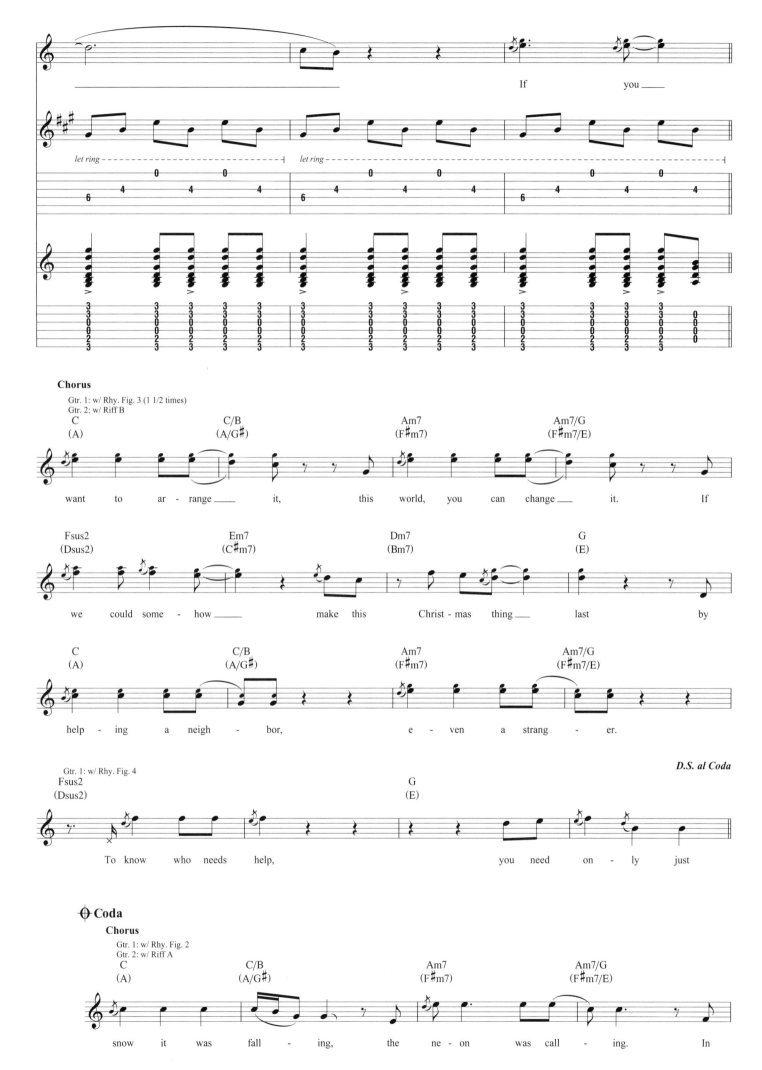

If you

Chorus

Gtr. 1: w/ Rhy. Fig. 3 (1 1/2 times)
Gtr. 2: w/ Riff B

C   C/B   Am7   Am7/G
(A)   (A/G#)   (F#m7)   (F#m7/E)

want   to   ar - range _____ it,   this world, you can change _____ it.   If

Fsus2   Em7   Dm7   G
(Dsus2)   (C#m7)   (Bm7)   (E)

we could some - how _____   make this Christ - mas thing _____ last   by

C   C/B   Am7   Am7/G
(A)   (A/G#)   (F#m7)   (F#m7/E)

help - ing a neigh - bor,   e - ven a strang - er.

D.S. al Coda

Gtr. 1: w/ Rhy. Fig. 4

Fsus2   G
(Dsus2)   (E)

To know   who needs help,   you need on - ly just

Coda

Chorus

Gtr. 1: w/ Rhy. Fig. 2
Gtr. 2: w/ Riff A

C   C/B   Am7   Am7/G
(A)   (A/G#)   (F#m7)   (F#m7/E)

snow it was fall - ing,   the ne - on was call - ing.   In

from Trans-Siberian Orchestra - *Beethoven's Last Night*

Requiem (The Fifth)

Music by Ludvig van Beethoven and W.A. Mozart
Arranged by Paul O'Neill

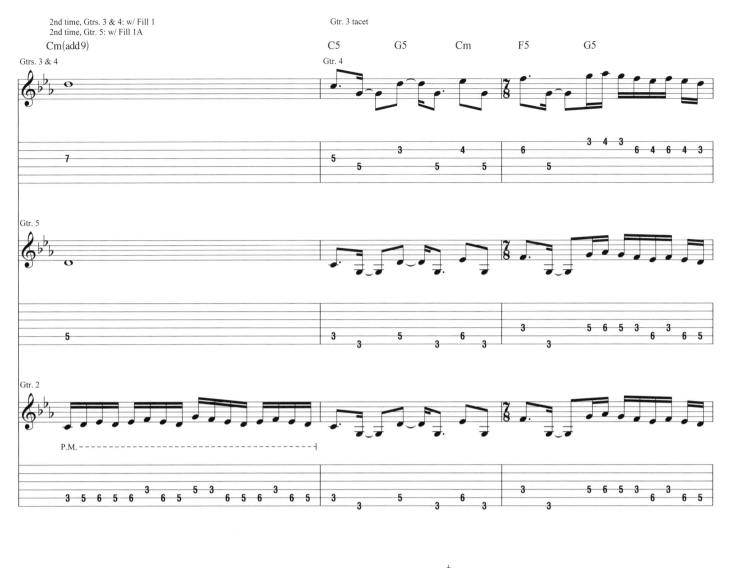

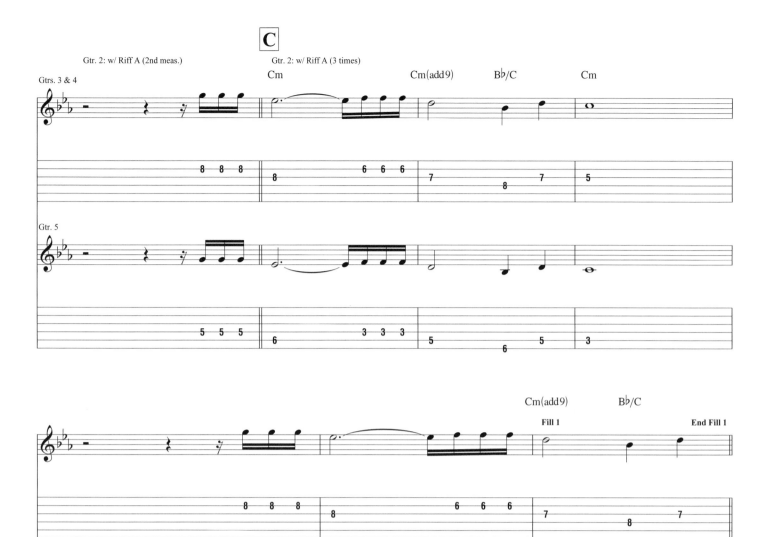

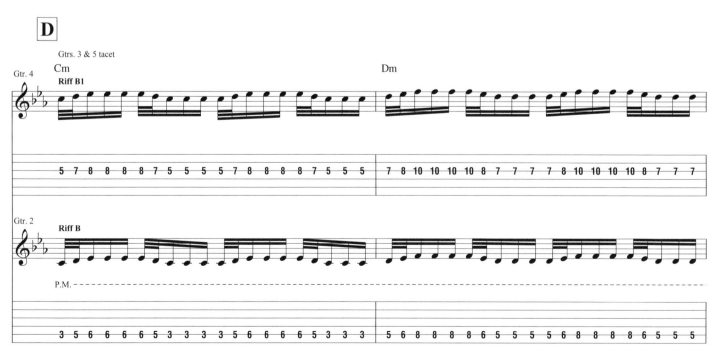

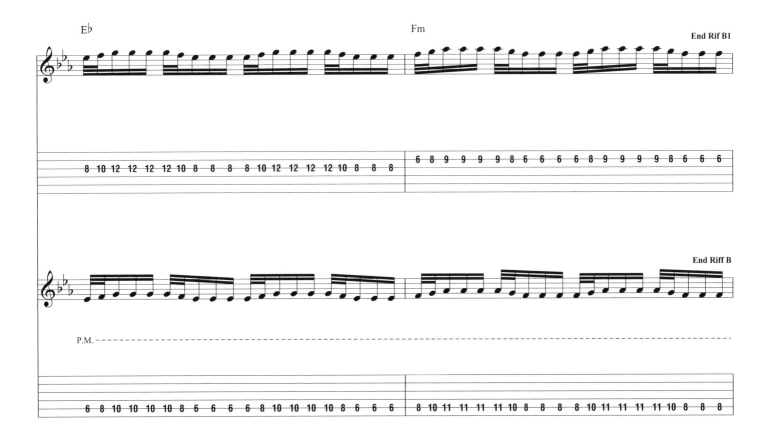

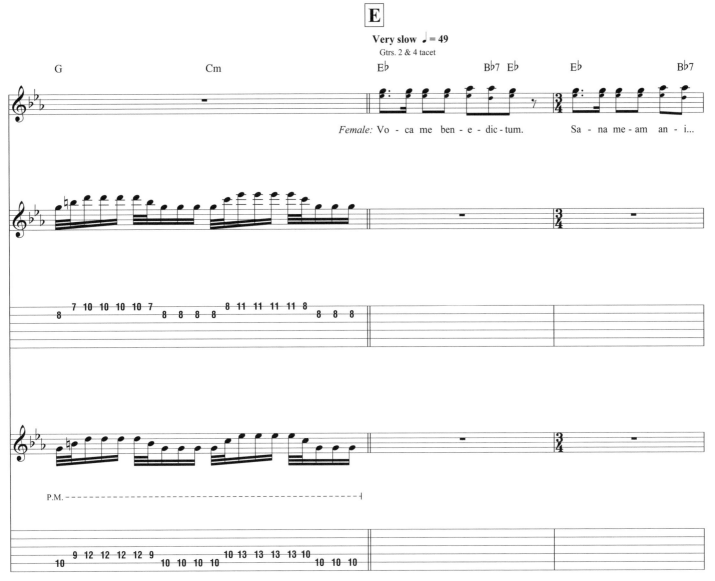

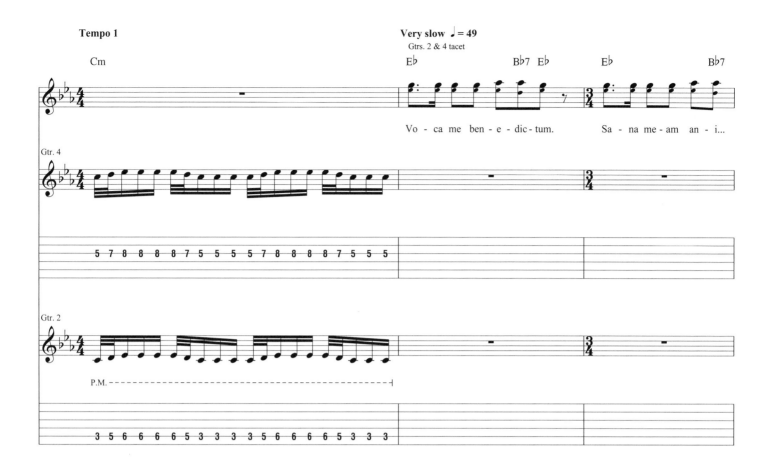

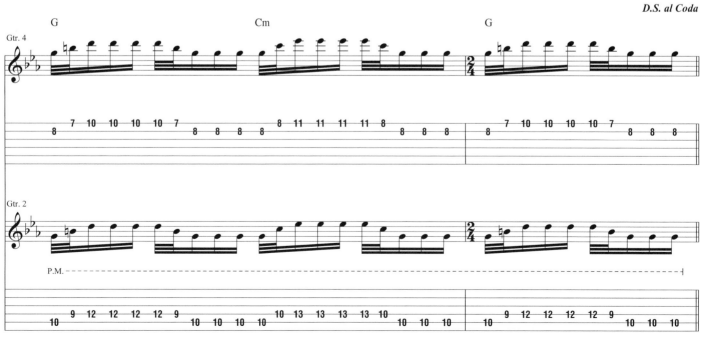

⊕ Coda

F

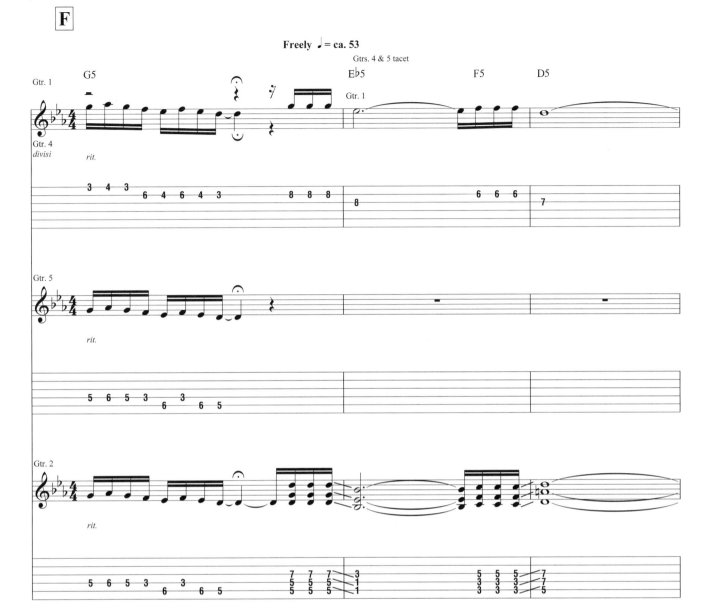

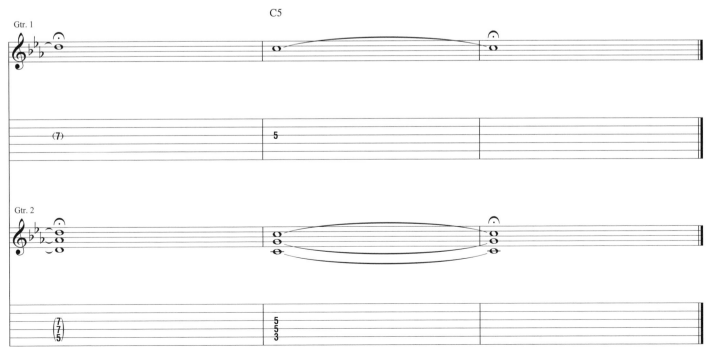

Siberian Sleigh Ride

Music by Paul O'Neill

C

Gtr. 2: w/ Riff A (3 1/2 times)

A7

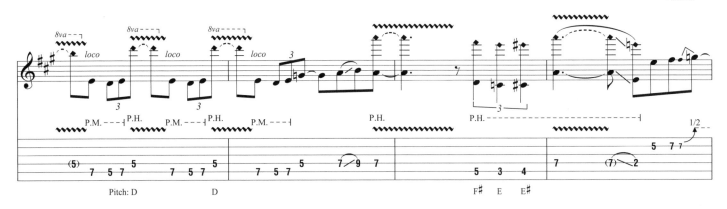

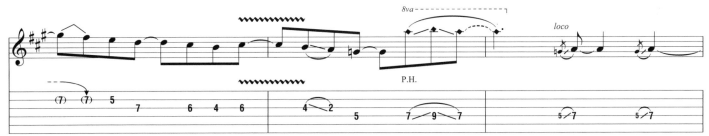

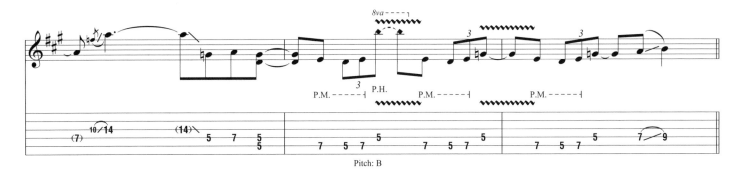

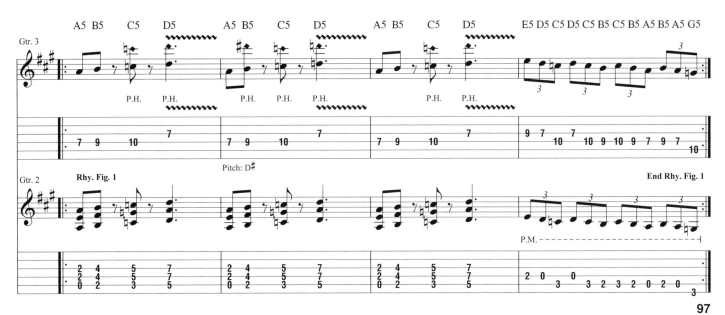

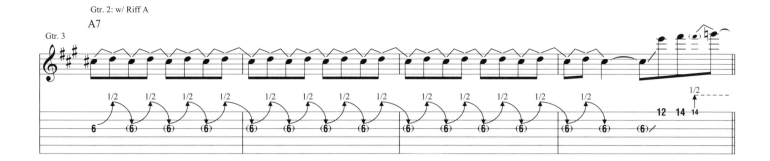

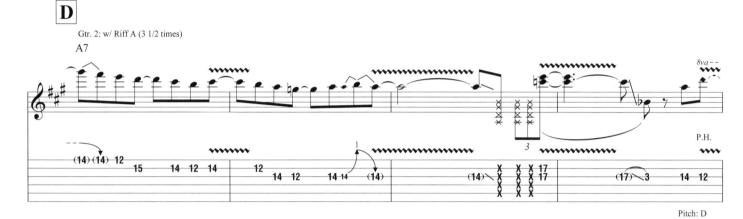

D

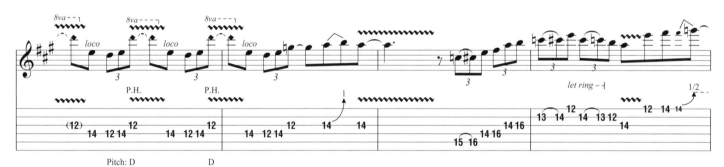

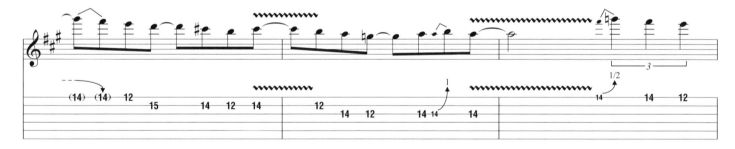

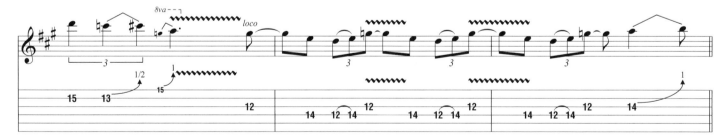

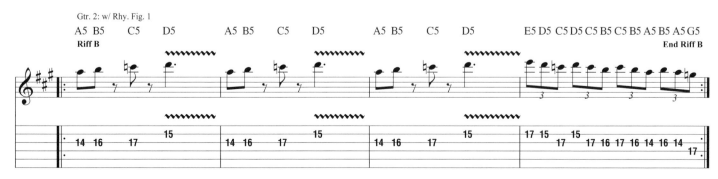

Gtr. 2: w/ Riff A

Aadd9

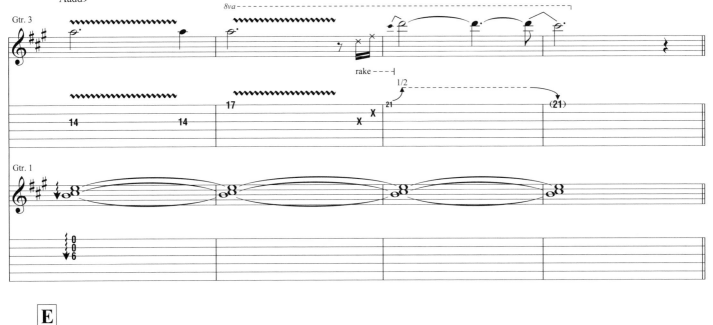

E

Gtr. 2: w/ Riff A (11 times)
Gtr. 3 tacet

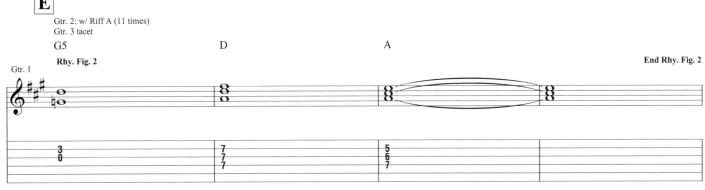

Gtr. 1: w/ Rhy. Fig. 2 (10 times)

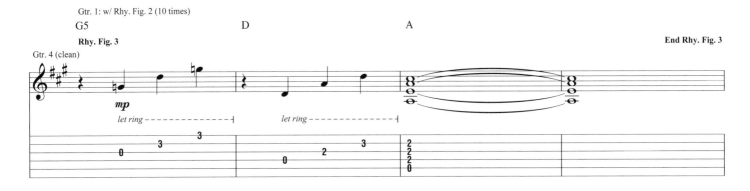

*Kybd. arr. for gtr.

Gtr. 4: w/ Rhy. Fig. 4
Gtr. 5: w/ Riff B

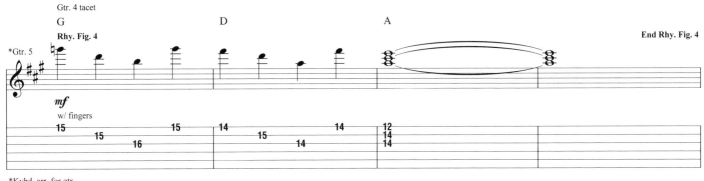

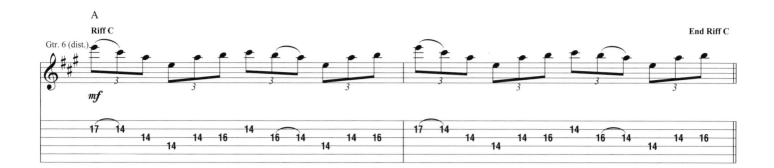

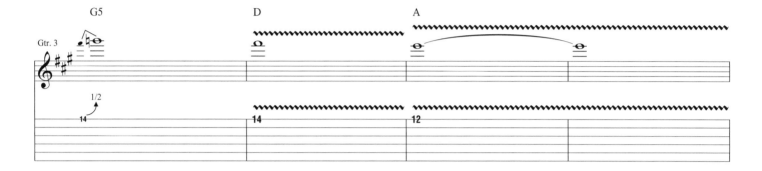

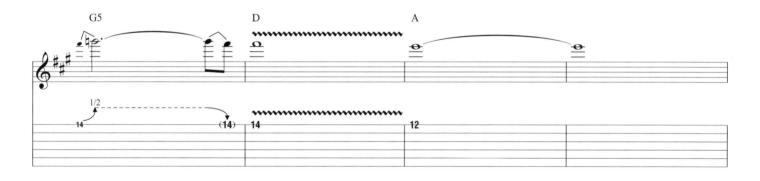

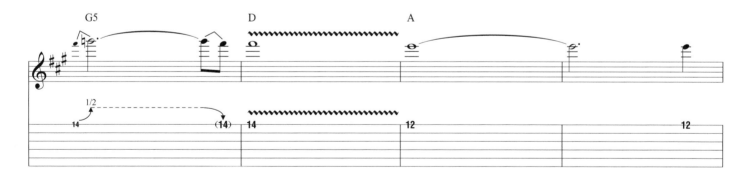

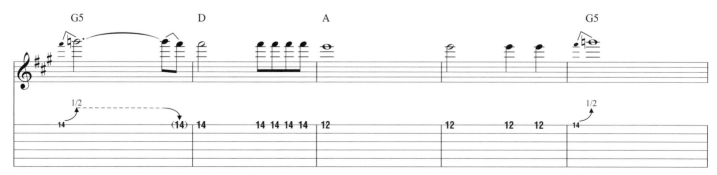

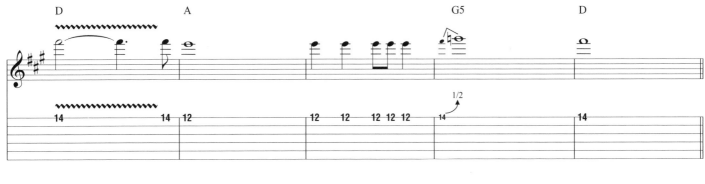

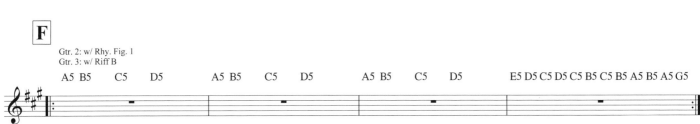

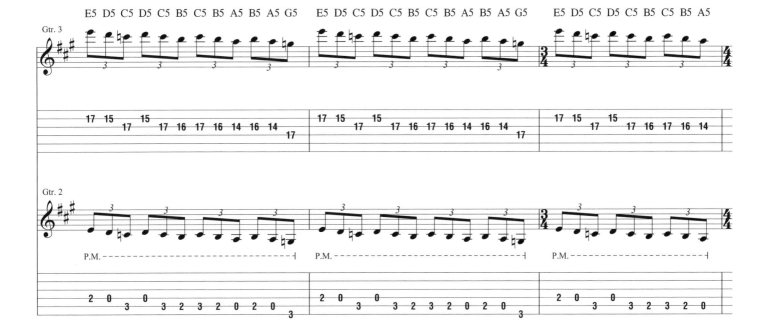

from Trans-Siberian Orchestra - *Night Castle*

Toccata-Carpimus Noctem

Music by J.S. Bach and Paul O'Neill

*String ensemble arr. for gtr.

**Doubled throughout

***Chord symbols reflect implied harmony.

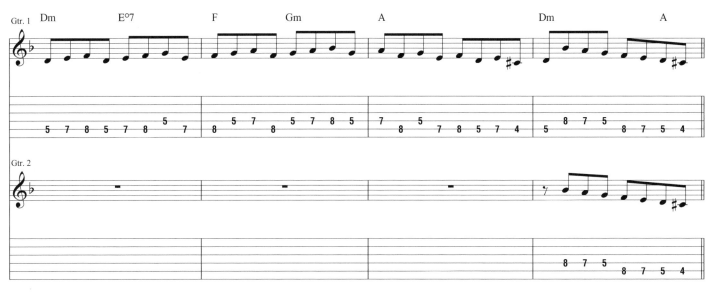

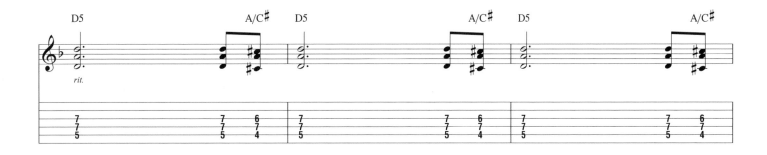

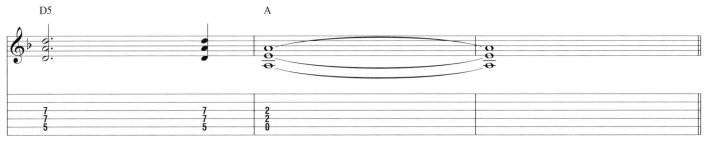

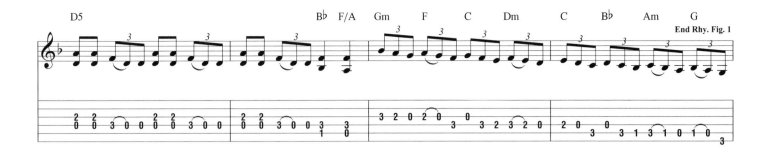

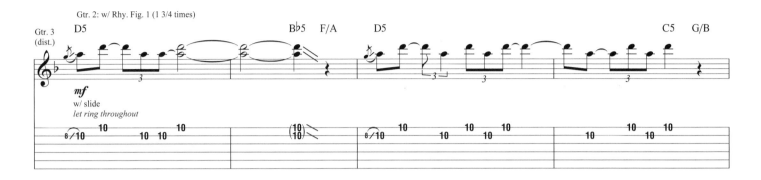

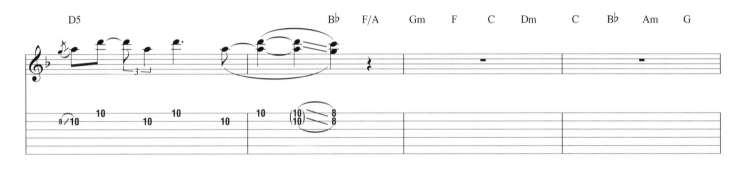

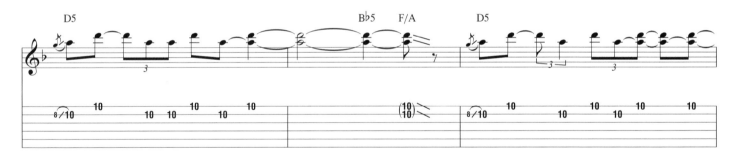

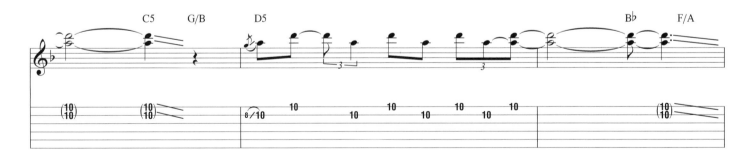

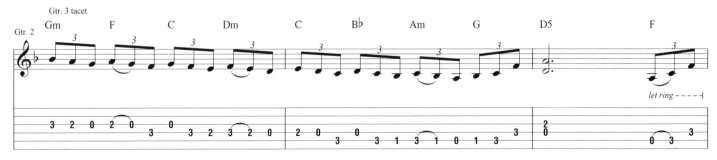

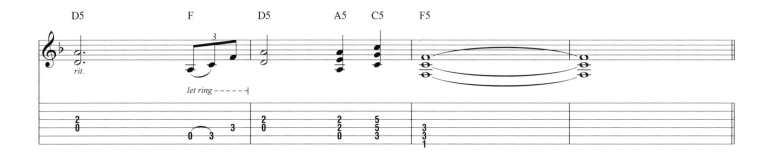

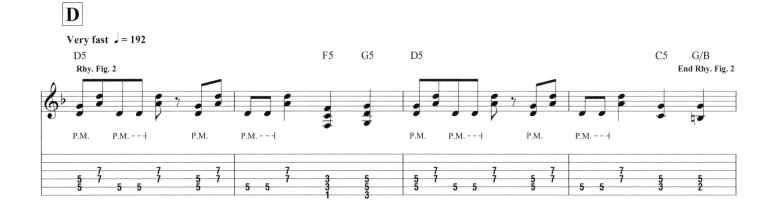

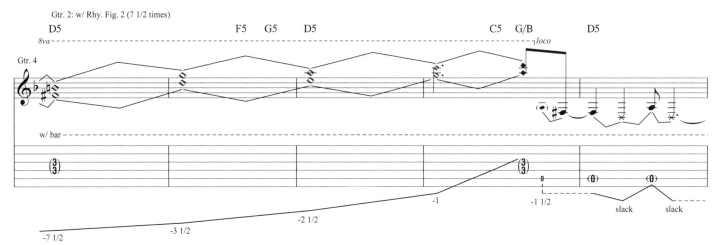

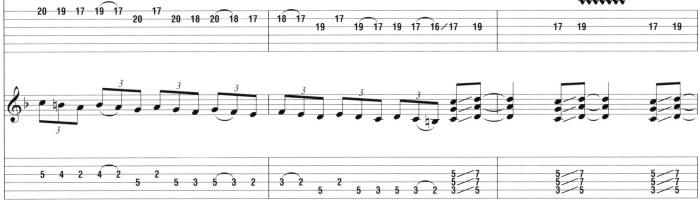

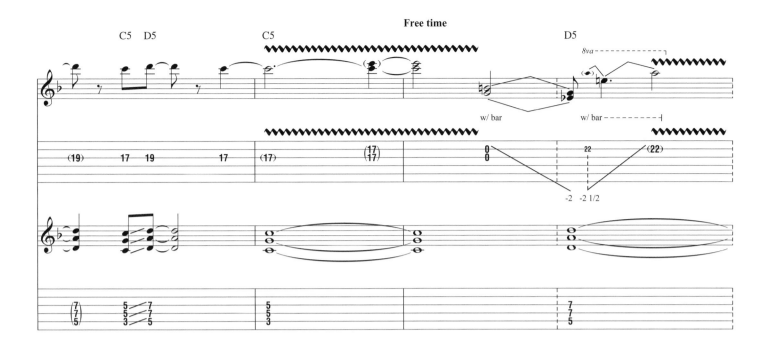

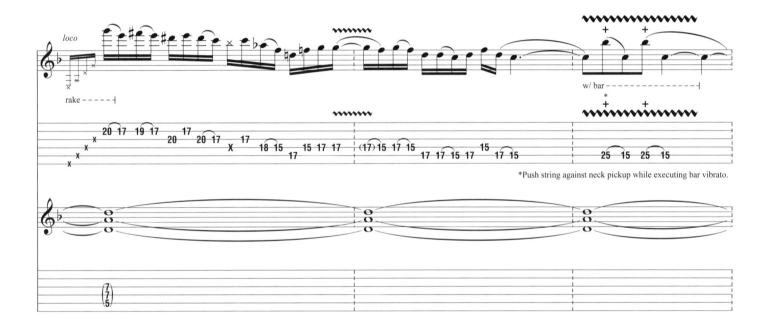

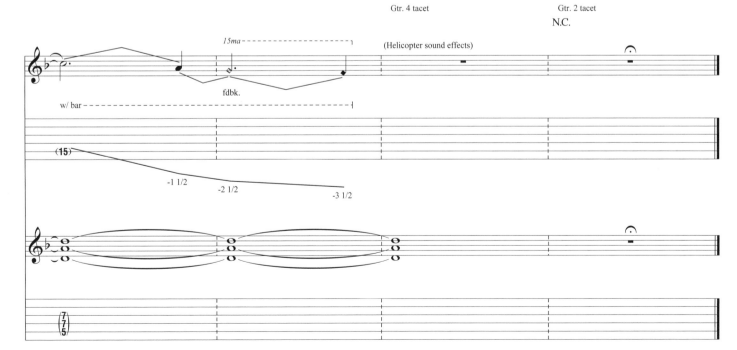

Wizards in Winter

Music by Paul O'Neill and Robert Kinkel

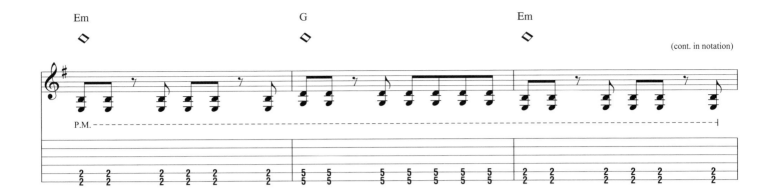

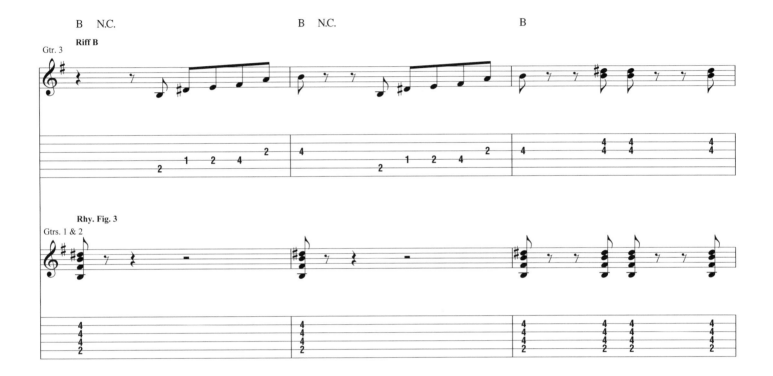

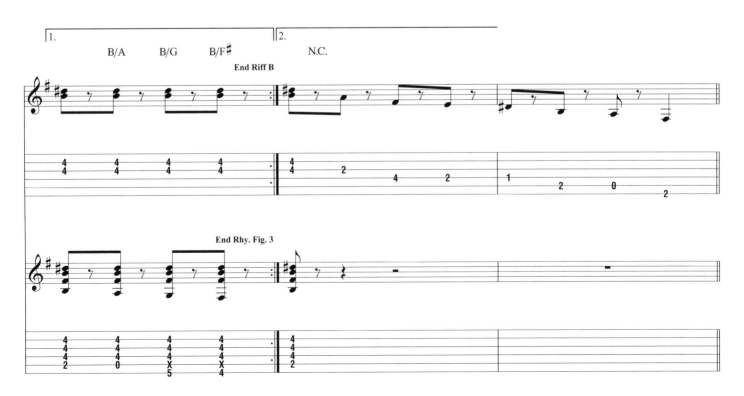

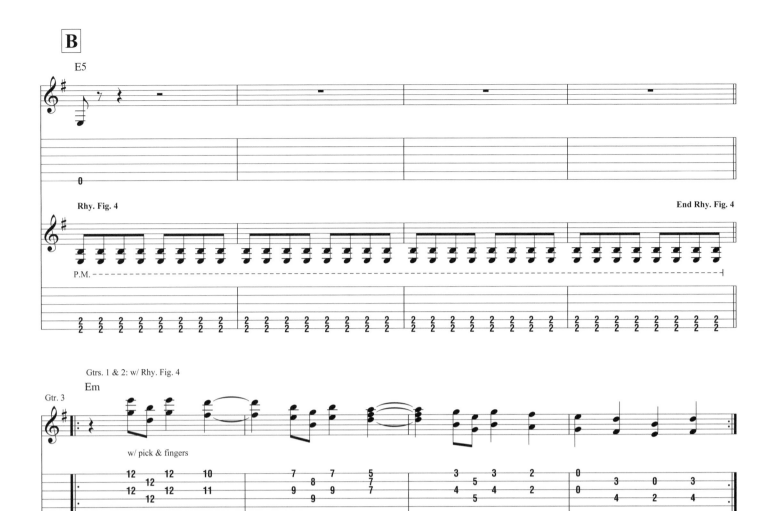

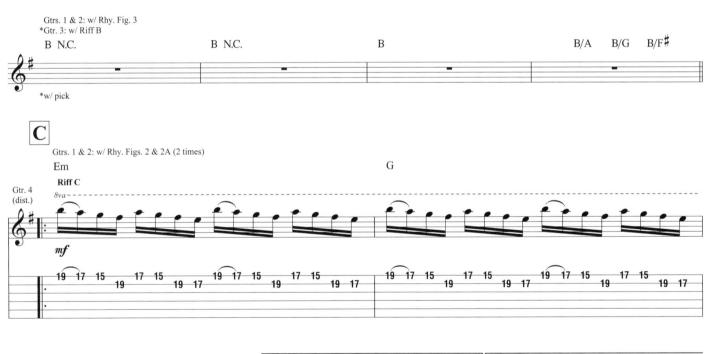

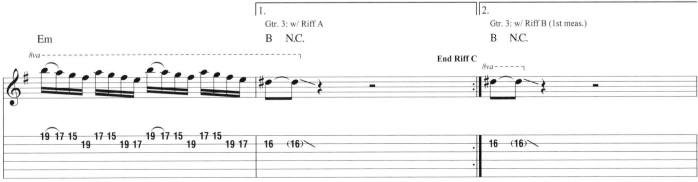

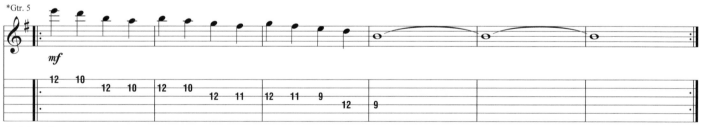
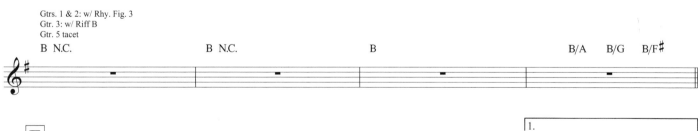

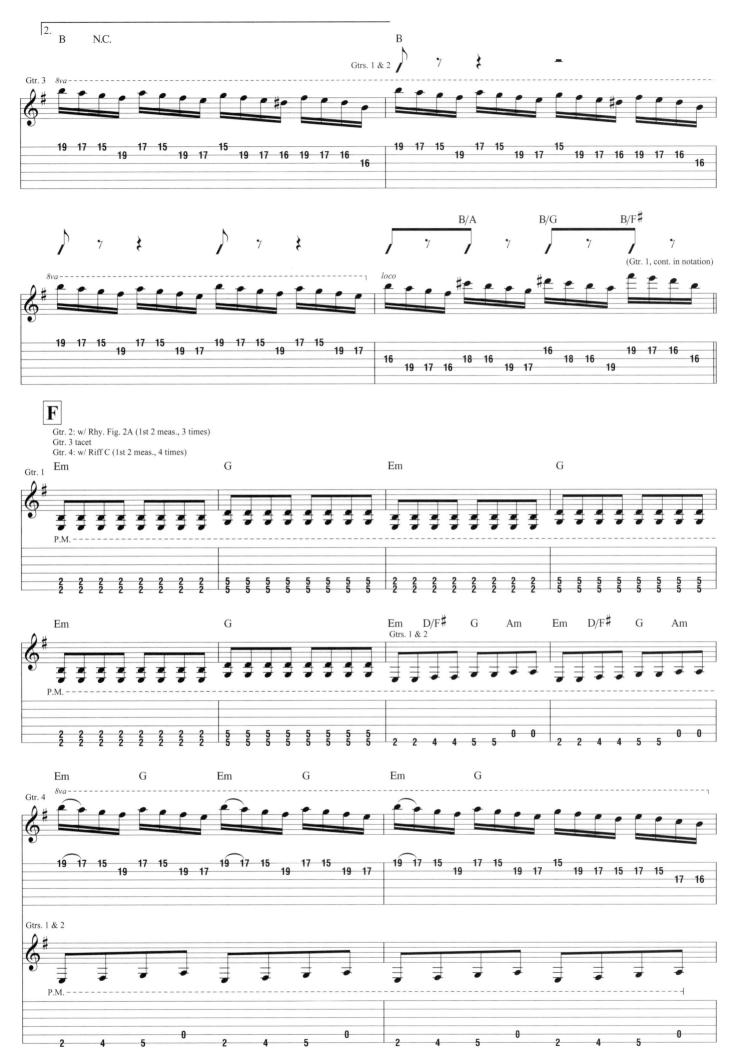

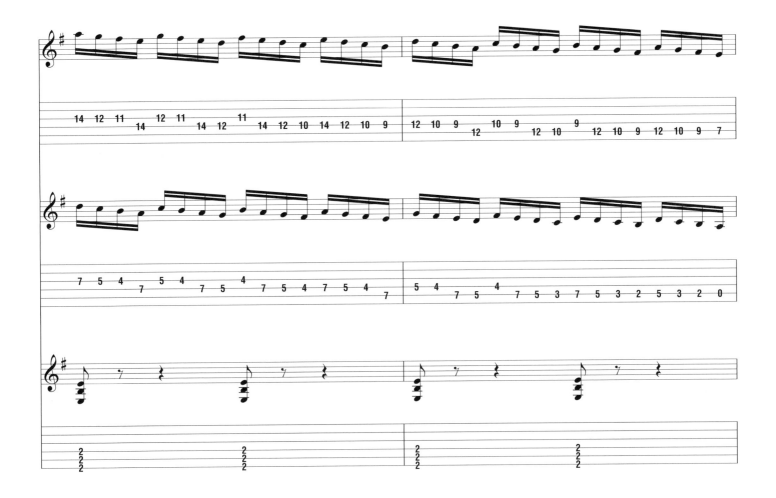

N.C.

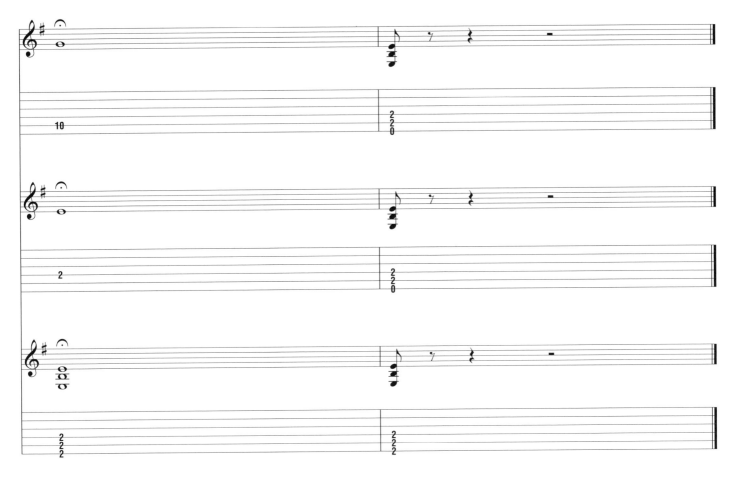

GUITAR NOTATION LEGEND

Guitar music can be notated three different ways: on a *musical staff*, in *tablature*, and in *rhythm slashes*.

RHYTHM SLASHES are written above the staff. Strum chords in the rhythm indicated. Use the chord diagrams found at the top of the first page of the transcription for the appropriate chord voicings. Round noteheads indicate single notes.

THE MUSICAL STAFF shows pitches and rhythms and is divided by bar lines into measures. Pitches are named after the first seven letters of the alphabet.

TABLATURE graphically represents the guitar fingerboard. Each horizontal line represents a string, and each number represents a fret.

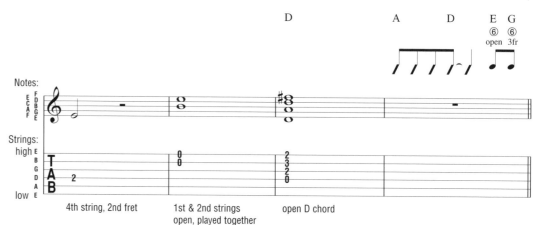

4th string, 2nd fret   1st & 2nd strings open, played together   open D chord

Definitions for Special Guitar Notation

HALF-STEP BEND: Strike the note and bend up 1/2 step.

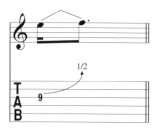

WHOLE-STEP BEND: Strike the note and bend up one step.

GRACE NOTE BEND: Strike the note and immediately bend up as indicated.

SLIGHT (MICROTONE) BEND: Strike the note and bend up 1/4 step.

BEND AND RELEASE: Strike the note and bend up as indicated, then release back to the original note. Only the first note is struck.

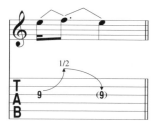

PRE-BEND: Bend the note as indicated, then strike it.

PRE-BEND AND RELEASE: Bend the note as indicated. Strike it and release the bend back to the original note.

UNISON BEND: Strike the two notes simultaneously and bend the lower note up to the pitch of the higher.

VIBRATO: The string is vibrated by rapidly bending and releasing the note with the fretting hand.

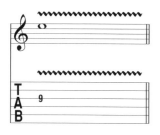

WIDE VIBRATO: The pitch is varied to a greater degree by vibrating with the fretting hand.

HAMMER-ON: Strike the first (lower) note with one finger, then sound the higher note (on the same string) with another finger by fretting it without picking.

PULL-OFF: Place both fingers on the notes to be sounded. Strike the first note and without picking, pull the finger off to sound the second (lower) note.

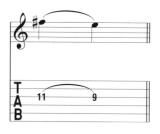

LEGATO SLIDE: Strike the first note and then slide the same fret-hand finger up or down to the second note. The second note is not struck.

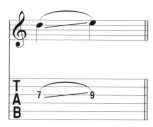

SHIFT SLIDE: Same as legato slide, except the second note is struck.

TRILL: Very rapidly alternate between the notes indicated by continuously hammering on and pulling off.

TAPPING: Hammer ("tap") the fret indicated with the pick-hand index or middle finger and pull off to the note fretted by the fret hand.

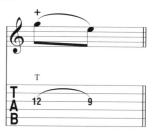

NATURAL HARMONIC: Strike the note while the fret-hand lightly touches the string directly over the fret indicated.

PINCH HARMONIC: The note is fretted normally and a harmonic is produced by adding the edge of the thumb or the tip of the index finger of the pick hand to the normal pick attack.

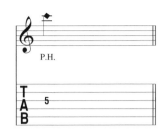

HARP HARMONIC: The note is fretted normally and a harmonic is produced by gently resting the pick hand's index finger directly above the indicated fret (in parentheses) while the pick hand's thumb or pick assists by plucking the appropriate string.

PICK SCRAPE: The edge of the pick is rubbed down (or up) the string, producing a scratchy sound.

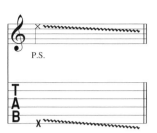

MUFFLED STRINGS: A percussive sound is produced by laying the fret hand across the string(s) without depressing, and striking them with the pick hand.

PALM MUTING: The note is partially muted by the pick hand lightly touching the string(s) just before the bridge.

RAKE: Drag the pick across the strings indicated with a single motion.

TREMOLO PICKING: The note is picked as rapidly and continuously as possible.

ARPEGGIATE: Play the notes of the chord indicated by quickly rolling them from bottom to top.

VIBRATO BAR DIVE AND RETURN: The pitch of the note or chord is dropped a specified number of steps (in rhythm), then returned to the original pitch.

VIBRATO BAR SCOOP: Depress the bar just before striking the note, then quickly release the bar.

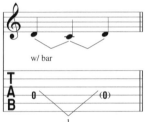

VIBRATO BAR DIP: Strike the note and then immediately drop a specified number of steps, then release back to the original pitch.

Additional Musical Definitions

(accent)	•	Accentuate note (play it louder).
(accent)	•	Accentuate note with great intensity.
(staccato)	•	Play the note short.
⊓	•	Downstroke
∨	•	Upstroke

Rhy. Fig. • Label used to recall a recurring accompaniment pattern (usually chordal).

Riff • Label used to recall composed, melodic lines (usually single notes) which recur.

Fill • Label used to identify a brief melodic figure which is to be inserted into the arrangement.

Rhy. Fill • A chordal version of a Fill.

tacet • Instrument is silent (drops out).

D.S. al Coda • Go back to the sign (𝄋), then play until the measure marked "*To Coda*," then skip to the section labelled "**Coda**."

D.C. al Fine • Go back to the beginning of the song and play until the measure marked "*Fine*" (end).

• Repeat measures between signs.

• When a repeated section has different endings, play the first ending only the first time and the second ending only the second time.

NOTE: Tablature numbers in parentheses mean:
1. The note is being sustained over a system (note in standard notation is tied), or
2. The note is sustained, but a new articulation (such as a hammer-on, pull-off, slide or vibrato) begins, or
3. The note is a barely audible "ghost" note (note in standard notation is also in parentheses).

GUITAR RECORDED VERSIONS®

AUTHENTIC TRANSCRIPTIONS WITH NOTES AND TABLATURE

Guitar Recorded Versions® are note-for-note transcriptions of guitar music taken directly off recordings. This series, one of the most popular in print today, features some of the greatest guitar players and groups from blues and rock to country and jazz.

Guitar Recorded Versions are transcribed by the best transcribers in the business. Every book contains notes and tablature. Visit **www.halleonard.com** for our complete selection.

14041344	The Definitive AC/DC Songbook	$39.99
00690016	The Will Ackerman Collection	$19.95
00690501	Bryan Adams – Greatest Hits	$19.95
00690603	Aerosmith – O Yeah! (Ultimate Hits)	$24.95
00690147	Aerosmith – Rocks	$19.95
00690178	Alice in Chains – Acoustic	$19.95
00694865	Alice in Chains – Dirt	$19.95
00660225	Alice in Chains – Facelift	$19.95
00694925	Alice in Chains – Jar of Flies/Sap	$19.95
00690387	Alice in Chains – Nothing Safe: Best of the Box	$19.95
00694932	Allman Brothers Band – Definitive Collection for Guitar Volume 1	$24.95
00694933	Allman Brothers Band – Definitive Collection for Guitar Volume 2	$24.95
00694934	Allman Brothers Band – Definitive Collection for Guitar Volume 3	$24.95
00690958	Duane Allman Guitar Anthology	$24.99
00691071	Alter Bridge – AB III	$22.99
00690945	Alter Bridge – Blackbird	$22.99
00690755	Alter Bridge – One Day Remains	$22.99
00123558	Arctic Monkeys – AM	$22.99
00114564	As I Lay Dying – Awakened	$22.99
00690158	Chet Atkins – Almost Alone	$19.95
00694876	Chet Atkins – Contemporary Styles	$19.95
00694878	Chet Atkins – Vintage Fingerstyle	$19.95
00690609	Audioslave	$19.95
00690804	Audioslave – Out of Exile	$19.95
00690884	Audioslave – Revelations	$19.95
00690926	Avenged Sevenfold	$22.95
00690820	Avenged Sevenfold – City of Evil	$24.95
00123216	Avenged Sevenfold – Hail to the King	$22.99
00691065	Avenged Sevenfold – Waking the Fallen	$22.99
00123140	The Avett Brothers Guitar Collection	$22.99
00694918	Randy Bachman Collection	$22.95
00690503	Beach Boys – Very Best of	$19.95
00694929	Beatles: 1962-1966	$24.99
00694930	Beatles: 1967-1970	$24.95
00690489	Beatles – 1	$24.99
00694880	Beatles – Abbey Road	$19.95
00691066	Beatles – Beatles for Sale	$22.99
00690110	Beatles – Book 1 (White Album)	$19.95
00690111	Beatles – Book 2 (White Album)	$19.95
00690902	Beatles – The Capitol Albums, Volume 1	$24.99
00694832	Beatles – For Acoustic Guitar	$22.99
00691031	Beatles – Help!	$19.99
00690482	Beatles – Let It Be	$17.95
00691067	Beatles – Meet the Beatles!	$22.99
00691068	Beatles – Please Please Me	$22.99
00694891	Beatles – Revolver	$19.95
00694914	Beatles – Rubber Soul	$22.99
00694863	Beatles – Sgt. Pepper's Lonely Hearts Club Band	$22.99
00110193	Beatles – Tomorrow Never Knows	$22.99
00691044	Jeff Beck – Best of Beck	$24.99
00690632	Beck – Sea Change	$19.95
00691041	Jeff Beck – Truth	$19.99
00694884	Best of George Benson	$19.95
00692385	Chuck Berry	$22.99
00690835	Billy Talent	$19.95
00690879	Billy Talent II	$19.95
00129737	The Black Keys – Turn Blue	$22.99
00690149	Black Sabbath	$16.99
00690901	Best of Black Sabbath	$19.95
00691010	Black Sabbath – Heaven and Hell	$22.99
00690148	Black Sabbath – Master of Reality	$16.99
00690142	Black Sabbath – Paranoid	$16.99
14042759	Black Sabbath – 13	$19.99
00692200	Black Sabbath – We Sold Our Soul for Rock 'N' Roll	$19.95
00690389	blink-182 – Enema of the State	$19.95
00690831	blink-182 – Greatest Hits	$19.95
00691179	blink-182 – Neighborhoods	$22.99
00690523	blink-182 – Take Off Your Pants and Jacket	$19.95
00690028	Blue Oyster Cult – Cult Classics	$19.95
00690008	Bon Jovi – Cross Road	$19.95
00691074	Bon Jovi – Greatest Hits	$22.99
00139086	Joe Bonamassa – Different Shades of Blue	$22.99
00690913	Boston	$19.95
00690829	Boston Guitar Collection	$19.99
00690491	Best of David Bowie	$19.95
00690583	Box Car Racer	$19.95
00691023	Breaking Benjamin – Dear Agony	$22.99
00690873	Breaking Benjamin – Phobia	$19.95
00690764	Breaking Benjamin – We Are Not Alone	$19.95
00690451	Jeff Buckley Collection	$24.95
00690957	Bullet for My Valentine – Scream Aim Fire	$22.99
00119629	Bullet for My Valentine – Temper Temper	$22.99
00690678	Best of Kenny Burrell	$19.95
00691077	Cage the Elephant – Thank You, Happy Birthday	$22.99
00691159	The Cars – Complete Greatest Hits	$22.99
00690261	Carter Family Collection	$19.95
00691079	Best of Johnny Cash	$22.99
00690043	Best of Cheap Trick	$19.95
00690171	Chicago – The Definitive Guitar Collection	$22.95
00691011	Chimaira Guitar Collection	$24.99
00690567	Charlie Christian – The Definitive Collection	$19.95
00101916	Eric Church – Chief	$22.99
00129545	The Civil Wars	$19.99
00138731	Eric Clapton & Friends – The Breeze	$22.99
00690590	Eric Clapton – Anthology	$29.95
00692391	Best of Eric Clapton – 2nd Edition	$22.95
00691055	Eric Clapton – Clapton	$22.99
00690936	Eric Clapton – Complete Clapton	$29.99
00690247	Eric Clapton – 461 Ocean Boulevard	$19.99
00690010	Eric Clapton – From the Cradle	$19.95
00690363	Eric Clapton – Just One Night	$24.99
00694873	Eric Clapton – Timepieces	$19.95
00694869	Eric Clapton – Unplugged	$22.95
00690415	Clapton Chronicles – Best of Eric Clapton	$18.95
00694896	John Mayall/Eric Clapton – Bluesbreakers	$19.95
00690162	Best of the Clash	$19.95
00690828	Coheed & Cambria – Good Apollo I'm Burning Star, IV, Vol. 1: From Fear Through the Eyes of Madness	$19.95
00690940	Coheed and Cambria – No World for Tomorrow	$19.95
00130786	Coldplay – Ghost Stories	$19.99
00690494	Coldplay – Parachutes	$19.95
00690593	Coldplay – A Rush of Blood to the Head	$19.95
00690806	Coldplay – X & Y	$19.95
00690855	Best of Collective Soul	$19.95
00691091	The Best of Alice Cooper	$22.99
00694940	Counting Crows – August & Everything After	$19.95
00127184	Best of Robert Cray	$19.99
00694840	Cream – Disraeli Gears	$19.95
00690285	Cream – Those Were the Days	$17.95
00690819	Best of Creedence Clearwater Revival	$22.95
00690648	The Very Best of Jim Croce	$19.95
00690572	Steve Cropper – Soul Man	$19.95
00690613	Best of Crosby, Stills & Nash	$22.95
00699521	The Cure – Greatest Hits	$24.95
00690637	Best of Dick Dale	$19.95
00690822	Best of Alex De Grassi	$19.95
00690967	Death Cab for Cutie – Narrow Stairs	$22.99
00690289	Best of Deep Purple	$19.99
00690288	Deep Purple – Machine Head	$17.99
00690784	Best of Def Leppard	$22.99
00694831	Derek and the Dominos – Layla & Other Assorted Love Songs	$22.95
00692240	Bo Diddley – Guitar Solos by Fred Sokolow	$19.99
00690384	Best of Ani DiFranco	$19.95
00690380	Ani DiFranco – Up Up Up Up Up Up	$19.95
00690979	Best of Dinosaur Jr.	$19.99
00690833	Private Investigations – Best of Dire Straits and Mark Knopfler	$24.95
00695382	Very Best of Dire Straits – Sultans of Swing	$22.95
00122443	Dream Theater	$24.99
00690250	Best of Duane Eddy	$16.95
00690909	Best of Tommy Emmanuel	$22.99
00690555	Best of Melissa Etheridge	$19.95
00690515	Extreme II – Pornograffitti	$19.95
00691009	Five Finger Death Punch	$19.99
00690664	Best of Fleetwood Mac	$19.95
00690870	Flyleaf	$19.95
00690808	Foo Fighters – In Your Honor	$19.95
00691115	Foo Fighters – Wasting Light	$22.99
00690805	Best of Robben Ford	$22.99
00120220	Robben Ford – Guitar Anthology	$24.99
00690842	Best of Peter Frampton	$19.95
00694920	Best of Free	$19.95
00694807	Danny Gatton – 88 Elmira St.	$19.95
00690438	Genesis Guitar Anthology	$19.95
00690753	Best of Godsmack	$19.95
00120167	Godsmack	$19.95
00690338	Goo Goo Dolls – Dizzy Up the Girl	$19.95
00113073	Green Day – Uno	$21.99
00116846	Green Day – ¡Dos!	$21.99
00118259	Green Day – ¡Tré!	$21.99
00691190	Best of Peter Green	$19.99
00690927	Patty Griffin – Children Running Through	$19.95
00690591	Patty Griffin – Guitar Collection	$19.95
00690978	Guns N' Roses – Chinese Democracy	$24.99
00691027	Buddy Guy Anthology	$24.99
00694854	Buddy Guy – Damn Right, I've Got the Blues	$19.95
00690697	Best of Jim Hall	$19.95
00690840	Ben Harper – Both Sides of the Gun	$19.95
00691018	Ben Harper – Fight for Your Mind	$22.99
00694798	George Harrison Anthology	$19.95
00690841	Scott Henderson – Blues Guitar Collection	$19.95
00692930	Jimi Hendrix – Are You Experienced?	$24.95
00692931	Jimi Hendrix – Axis: Bold As Love	$22.95
00690304	Jimi Hendrix – Band of Gypsys	$24.99
00690608	Jimi Hendrix – Blue Wild Angel	$24.95
00694944	Jimi Hendrix – Blues	$24.95
00692932	Jimi Hendrix – Electric Ladyland	$24.95
00119619	Jimi Hendrix – People, Hell and Angels	$22.99
00690602	Jimi Hendrix – Smash Hits	$24.99
00691152	West Coast Seattle Boy: The Jimi Hendrix Anthology	$29.99
00691332	Jimi Hendrix – Winterland (Highlights)	$22.99
00690017	Jimi Hendrix – Woodstock	$24.95
00690843	H.I.M. – Dark Light	$19.95
00690869	Hinder – Extreme Behavior	$19.95
00660029	Buddy Holly	$22.99
00690793	John Lee Hooker Anthology	$24.99
00660169	John Lee Hooker – A Blues Legend	$19.95
00694905	Howlin' Wolf	$19.95
00690692	Very Best of Billy Idol	$19.95
00121961	Imagine Dragons – Night Visions	$22.99
00690688	Incubus – A Crow Left of the Murder	$19.95
00690136	Indigo Girls – 1200 Curfews	$22.95
00690790	Iron Maiden Anthology	$24.99
00691058	Iron Maiden – The Final Frontier	$22.99
00690887	Iron Maiden – A Matter of Life and Death	$24.95
00690730	Alan Jackson – Guitar Collection	$19.95
00694938	Elmore James – Master Electric Slide Guitar	$19.95
00690652	Best of Jane's Addiction	$19.95
00690684	Jethro Tull – Aqualung	$19.95
00690693	Jethro Tull Guitar Anthology	$22.99
00691182	Jethro Tull – Stand Up	$22.99
00690898	John 5 – The Devil Knows My Name	$22.95
00690814	John 5 – Songs for Sanity	$19.95
00690751	John 5 – Vertigo	$19.95
00694912	Eric Johnson – Ah Via Musicom	$19.95
00690660	Best of Eric Johnson	$22.99
00691076	Eric Johnson – Up Close	$22.99

00690169	Eric Johnson – Venus Isle	$22.95
00122439	Jack Johnson – From Here to Now to You	$22.99
00690846	Jack Johnson and Friends – Sing-A-Longs and Lullabies for the Film Curious George	$19.95
00690271	Robert Johnson – The New Transcriptions	$24.95
00699131	Best of Janis Joplin	$19.95
00690427	Best of Judas Priest	$22.99
00690277	Best of Kansas	$19.95
00690911	Best of Phil Keaggy	$24.99
00690727	Toby Keith Guitar Collection	$19.99
00120814	Killswitch Engage – Disarm the Descent	$22.99
00690504	Very Best of Albert King	$19.95
00124869	Albert King with Stevie Ray Vaughan – In Session	$22.99
00130447	B.B. King – Live at the Regal	$17.99
00690444	B.B. King & Eric Clapton – Riding with the King	$22.99
00690134	Freddie King Collection	$19.95
00691062	Kings of Leon – Come Around Sundown	$22.99
00690157	Kiss – Alive!	$19.95
00690356	Kiss – Alive II	$22.99
00694903	Best of Kiss for Guitar	$24.95
00690355	Kiss – Destroyer	$16.95
14026320	Mark Knopfler – Get Lucky	$22.99
00690164	Mark Knopfler Guitar – Vol. 1	$19.95
00690163	Mark Knopfler/Chet Atkins – Neck and Neck	$19.95
00690780	Korn – Greatest Hits, Volume 1	$22.95
00690377	Kris Kristofferson Collection	$19.95
00690834	Lamb of God – Ashes of the Wake	$19.95
00690875	Lamb of God – Sacrament	$19.95
00690977	Ray LaMontagne – Gossip in the Grain	$19.99
00690823	Ray LaMontagne – Trouble	$19.95
00691057	Ray LaMontagne and the Pariah Dogs – God Willin' & The Creek Don't Rise	$22.99
00690922	Linkin Park – Minutes to Midnight	$19.95
00699623	The Best of Chuck Loeb	$19.95
00114563	The Lumineers	$22.99
00690525	Best of George Lynch	$24.99
00690955	Lynyrd Skynyrd – All-Time Greatest Hits	$22.99
00694954	New Best of Lynyrd Skynyrd	$19.95
00690577	Yngwie Malmsteen – Anthology	$24.95
00690754	Marilyn Manson – Lest We Forget	$19.95
00694956	Bob Marley – Legend	$19.95
00690548	Very Best of Bob Marley & The Wailers – One Love	$22.99
00694945	Bob Marley – Songs of Freedom	$24.95
00690914	Maroon 5 – It Won't Be Soon Before Long	$19.95
00690657	Maroon 5 – Songs About Jane	$19.95
00690748	Maroon 5 – 1.22.03 Acoustic	$19.95
00690989	Mastodon – Crack the Skye	$24.99
00119220	Brent Mason – Hot Wired	$19.99
00691176	Mastodon – The Hunter	$22.99
00137718	Mastodon – Once More 'Round the Sun	$22.99
00690616	Matchbox Twenty – More Than You Think You Are	$19.95
00691942	Andy McKee – Art of Motion	$22.99
00691034	Andy McKee – Joyland	$19.99
00120080	The Don McLean Songbook	$19.95
00694952	Megadeth – Countdown to Extinction	$22.95
00690244	Megadeth – Cryptic Writings	$19.95
00694951	Megadeth – Rust in Peace	$22.95
00690011	Megadeth – Youthanasia	$22.99
00690505	John Mellencamp Guitar Collection	$19.95
00690562	Pat Metheny – Bright Size Life	$19.95
00691073	Pat Metheny with Christian McBride & Antonion Sanchez – Day Trip/Tokyo Day Trip Live	$22.99
00690646	Pat Metheny – One Quiet Night	$19.95
00690559	Pat Metheny – Question & Answer	$19.95
00118836	Pat Metheny – Unity Band	$22.99
00102590	Pat Metheny – What's It All About	$22.99
00690040	Steve Miller Band Greatest Hits	$19.95
00119338	Ministry Guitar Tab Collection	$24.99
00102591	Wes Montgomery Guitar Anthology	$24.99
00694802	Gary Moore – Still Got the Blues	$22.99
00691005	Best of Motion City Soundtrack	$19.99
00129884	Jason Mraz – Yes!	$22.99
00690787	Mudvayne – L.D. 50	$22.95
00691070	Mumford & Sons – Sigh No More	$22.99
00118196	Muse – The 2nd Law	$19.99
00690996	My Morning Jacket Collection	$19.99
00690984	Matt Nathanson – Some Mad Hope	$22.99
00690611	Nirvana	$22.95
00694895	Nirvana – Bleach	$19.95
00694913	Nirvana – In Utero	$19.95
00694883	Nirvana – Nevermind	$19.95
00690026	Nirvana – Unplugged in New York	$19.95
00120112	No Doubt – Tragic Kingdom	$22.95
00690226	Oasis – The Other Side of Oasis	$19.95
00307163	Oasis – Time Flies... 1994-2009	$19.99
00690818	The Best of Opeth	$22.95
00691052	Roy Orbison – Black & White Night	$22.99
00694847	Best of Ozzy Osbourne	$22.95
00690399	Ozzy Osbourne – The Ozzman Cometh	$22.99
00690933	Best of Brad Paisley	$22.95
00690995	Brad Paisley – Play: The Guitar Album	$24.99
00690939	Christopher Parkening – Solo Pieces	$19.99
00690594	Best of Les Paul	$19.95
00694855	Pearl Jam – Ten	$22.99
00690439	A Perfect Circle – Mer De Noms	$19.95
00690725	Best of Carl Perkins	$19.99
00690499	Tom Petty – Definitive Guitar Collection	$19.95
00690868	Tom Petty – Highway Companion	$19.95
00690176	Phish – Billy Breathes	$22.95
00691249	Phish – Junta	$22.99
00121933	Pink Floyd – Acoustic Guitar Collection	$22.99
00690428	Pink Floyd – Dark Side of the Moon	$19.95
00690789	Best of Poison	$19.95
00690299	Best of Elvis: The King of Rock 'n' Roll	$19.95
00692535	Elvis Presley	$19.95
00690925	The Very Best of Prince	$22.99
00690003	Classic Queen	$24.95
00694975	Queen – Greatest Hits	$24.95
00690670	Very Best of Queensryche	$19.95
00690878	The Raconteurs – Broken Boy Soldiers	$19.95
00109303	Radiohead Guitar Anthology	$24.99
00694910	Rage Against the Machine	$19.95
00119834	Rage Against the Machine – Guitar Anthology	$22.99
00690179	Rancid – And Out Come the Wolves	$22.95
00690426	Best of Ratt	$19.95
00690055	Red Hot Chili Peppers – Blood Sugar Sex Magik	$19.95
00690584	Red Hot Chili Peppers – By the Way	$19.95
00690379	Red Hot Chili Peppers – Californication	$19.95
00690673	Red Hot Chili Peppers – Greatest Hits	$19.95
00690090	Red Hot Chili Peppers – One Hot Minute	$22.95
00691166	Red Hot Chili Peppers – I'm with You	$22.99
00690852	Red Hot Chili Peppers – Stadium Arcadium	$24.95
00690511	Django Reinhardt – The Definitive Collection	$19.95
00690779	Relient K – MMHMM	$19.95
00690643	Relient K – Two Lefts Don't Make a Right ... But Three Do	$19.95
00690260	Jimmie Rodgers Guitar Collection	$19.95
00138485	Kid Rock – Guitar Tab Collection	$19.99
14041901	Rodrigo Y Gabriela and C.U.B.A. – Area 52	$24.99
00690014	Rolling Stones – Exile on Main Street	$24.95
00690631	Rolling Stones – Guitar Anthology	$27.95
00690685	David Lee Roth – Eat 'Em and Smile	$19.95
00690031	Santana's Greatest Hits	$19.95
00690796	Very Best of Michael Schenker	$19.95
00128870	Matt Schofield Guitar Tab Collection	$22.99
00690566	Best of Scorpions	$22.95
00690604	Bob Seger – Guitar Anthology	$22.99
00138870	Ed Sheeran – X	$19.99
00690803	Best of Kenny Wayne Shepherd Band	$19.95
00690750	Kenny Wayne Shepherd – The Place You're In	$19.95
00690857	Shinedown – Us and Them	$19.95
00122218	Skillet – Rise	$22.99
00691114	Slash – Guitar Anthology	$24.99
00690872	Slayer – Christ Illusion	$19.95
00690813	Slayer – Guitar Collection	$19.95
00690419	Slipknot	$19.95
00690973	Slipknot – All Hope Is Gone	$22.99
00690330	Social Distortion – Live at the Roxy	$19.95
00120004	Best of Steely Dan	$24.95
00694921	Best of Steppenwolf	$22.95
00690655	Best of Mike Stern	$19.95
14041588	Cat Stevens – Tea for the Tillerman	$19.99
00690949	Rod Stewart Guitar Anthology	$19.99
00690021	Sting – Fields of Gold	$19.95
00690520	Styx Guitar Collection	$19.95
00120081	Sublime	$19.95
00690992	Sublime – Robbin' the Hood	$19.99
00690519	SUM 41 – All Killer No Filler	$19.95
00691072	Best of Supertramp	$22.99
00690994	Taylor Swift	$22.99
00690993	Taylor Swift – Fearless	$22.99
00142151	Taylor Swift – 1989	$22.99
00115957	Taylor Swift – Red	$21.99
00691063	Taylor Swift – Speak Now	$22.99

RECORDED VERSIONS GUITAR®

AUTHENTIC TRANSCRIPTIONS WITH NOTES AND TABLATURE

00690767	Switchfoot – The Beautiful Letdown	$19.95
00690531	System of a Down – Toxicity	$19.95
00694824	Best of James Taylor	$17.99
00694887	Best of Thin Lizzy	$19.95
00690871	Three Days Grace – One-X	$19.95
00690891	30 Seconds to Mars – A Beautiful Lie	$19.95
00690233	The Merle Travis Collection	$19.99
00690683	Robin Trower – Bridge of Sighs	$19.95
00699191	U2 – Best of: 1980-1990	$19.95
00690732	U2 – Best of: 1990-2000	$19.95
00690894	U2 – 18 Singles	$19.95
00124461	Keith Urban – Guitar Anthology	$19.99
00690039	Steve Vai – Alien Love Secrets	$24.95
00690172	Steve Vai – Fire Garden	$24.95
00660137	Steve Vai – Passion & Warfare	$24.95
00690881	Steve Vai – Real Illusions: Reflections	$24.95
00694904	Steve Vai – Sex and Religion	$24.95
00110385	Steve Vai – The Story of Light	$22.99
00690392	Steve Vai – The Ultra Zone	$19.95
00700555	Van Halen – Van Halen	$19.99
00690024	Stevie Ray Vaughan – Couldn't Stand the Weather	$19.95
00690370	Stevie Ray Vaughan and Double Trouble – The Real Deal: Greatest Hits Volume 2	$22.95
00690116	Stevie Ray Vaughan – Guitar Collection	$24.95
00660136	Stevie Ray Vaughan – In Step	$19.95
00694879	Stevie Ray Vaughan – In the Beginning	$19.95
00660058	Stevie Ray Vaughan – Lightnin' Blues '83-'87	$24.95
00694835	Stevie Ray Vaughan – The Sky Is Crying	$22.95
00690025	Stevie Ray Vaughan – Soul to Soul	$19.95
00690015	Stevie Ray Vaughan – Texas Flood	$19.95
00690772	Velvet Revolver – Contraband	$22.95
00109770	Volbeat Guitar Collection	$22.99
00121808	Volbeat – Outlaw Gentlemen & Shady Ladies	$22.99
00690132	The T-Bone Walker Collection	$19.95
00694789	Muddy Waters – Deep Blues	$24.95
00690071	Weezer (The Blue Album)	$19.95
00690516	Weezer (The Green Album)	$19.95
00690286	Weezer – Pinkerton	$19.95
00691046	Weezer – Rarities Edition	$22.99
00117511	Whitesnake Guitar Collection	$19.99
00690447	Best of the Who	$24.95
00691941	The Who – Acoustic Guitar Collection	$22.99
00691006	Wilco Guitar Collection	$22.99
00690672	Best of Dar Williams	$19.95
00691017	Wolfmother – Cosmic Egg	$22.99
00690319	Stevie Wonder – Hits	$19.99
00690596	Best of the Yardbirds	$19.95
00690844	Yellowcard – Lights and Sounds	$19.95
00690916	The Best of Dwight Yoakam	$19.95
00691020	Neil Young – After the Goldrush	$22.99
00691019	Neil Young – Everybody Knows This Is Nowhere	$19.99
00690904	Neil Young – Harvest	$29.99
00691021	Neil Young – Harvest Moon	$22.99
00690905	Neil Young – Rust Never Sleeps	$19.99
00690443	Frank Zappa – Hot Rats	$19.95
00690624	Frank Zappa and the Mothers of Invention – One Size Fits All	$22.99
00690623	Frank Zappa – Over-Nite Sensation	$22.99
00121684	ZZ Top – Early Classics	$24.99
00690589	ZZ Top – Guitar Anthology	$24.95
00690960	ZZ Top Guitar Classics	$19.99

HAL•LEONARD® CORPORATION
7777 W. Bluemound Rd. P.O. Box 13819 Milwaukee, WI 53213

Complete songlists and more at **www.halleonard.com**

Prices, contents, and availability subject to change without notice.

0515